PRAISE FOR

BREATHING OUT

"More Black women are coming out of hiding to share their truths about how racism is making them sick. Whitney Parnell is one of them. In *Breathing Out: Ruminations of a Millennial Black Woman*, she takes us across the globe as a Foreign Service kid, where she experienced the harshest forms of racism. In the United States, she takes us into nonprofit organizations where she cut her teeth to develop and lead professionally. In each setting, she reveals heart-breaking stories of navigating whiteness, the costs of doing so, and the scars that remain. This book is for allies who need to know, and BIPOC women who already do. This book is for everyone with a mission to end racism."

DR. YANIQUE REDWOOD, author of *White Women Cry and Call Me Angry: A Black Woman's Memoir on Racism in Philanthropy*

"I'm grateful to call Whitney Parnell a friend, a consummate ally, and a tireless champion for racial justice. In this time filled with racial backlash and retrenchment, *Breathing Out* provides a provocative road map and call to action to embrace and advance anti-racism and equity as both a moral and civic imperative."

ADAM RUSSELL TAYLOR, president of *Sojourners* magazine and author of *A More Perfect Union: A New Vision for Building the Beloved Community*

"In clear, accessible, and deeply moving prose, Whitney Parnell lays out the daily toll of navigating whiteness. Through recognizable examples of interpersonal and workplace dynamics, she illuminates its machinations. In so doing, she offers her readers a view into the inevitable role each of us plays—in either protecting or interrupting—systemic racism. For white readers, consider this your handbook for aligning professed anti-racist commitments with actual anti-racist practice."

ROBIN DIANGELO, bestselling author of *White Fragility*

"I met Whitney Parnell when she was doing training for *Sojourners*, and we have been talking ever since. This young leader embodies the struggle of Black millennial women. This is her story, and it is one that we must truly hear and understand for the future of this country, which strong Black women like Whitney will help to lead."

JIM WALLIS, founder of *Sojourners* magazine and author of *America's Original Sin: Racism, White Privilege, and the Bridge to a New America* and *The False White Gospel: Rejecting Christian Nationalism, Reclaiming True Faith, and Refounding Democracy*

BREATHING OUT

MASCOT BOOKS
an imprint of Amplify Publishing Group

www.mascotbooks.com

Breathing Out: Ruminations of a Millennial Black Woman

The author has tried to recreate events, locales, and conversations from their memories of them. In order to maintain their anonymity in some instances, the author has changed the names of individuals and places, and may have changed some identifying characteristics and details such as physical properties, occupations, and places of residence. The publisher and the author assume no responsibility for errors, inaccuracies, omissions, or any other inconsistencies herein. All such instances are unintentional and the author's own.

For more information, please contact:
Mascot Books, an imprint of Amplify Publishing Group
620 Herndon Parkway, Suite 220
Herndon, VA 20170
info@mascotbooks.com

Library of Congress Control Number: 2024913165
CPSIA Code: PRV0825A
ISBN-13: 979-8-89138-211-4

Printed in the United States

For my parents, whose boundless love, support, and sacrifice have enabled me to live my best life, and for my sisters, whose infinite friendship always keeps me full.

BREATHING OUT

RUMINATIONS OF A MILLENNIAL BLACK WOMAN

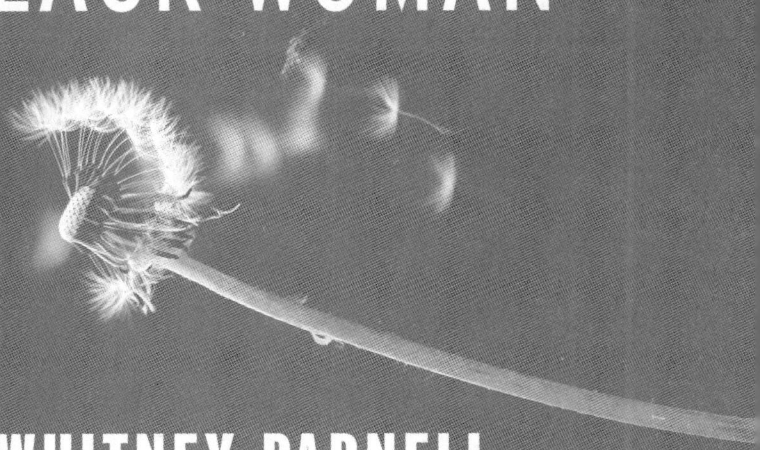

WHITNEY PARNELL

MASCOT BOOKS
an imprint of Amplify Publishing Group

CONTENTS

FOREWORD by Mary-Frances Winters 1

INTRODUCTION 5

PART ONE: MY PHILOSOPHY

Chapter 1 • **My Life** 13

Chapter 2 • **My Evolution** 17

Chapter 3 • **My Age** 21

PART TWO: YES, WE ARE CENTERING RACE

Part Two • **Introduction** 27

Chapter 4 • **The Truth** 31

Chapter 5 • **The Morphing** 39

Chapter 6 • **The Irrelevance of Relativity** 55

Chapter 7 • **The Neutrality** 63

PART THREE: NAVIGATING WHITENESS

Part Three • **Introduction** 71

Chapter 8 • **Scars** 75

Chapter 9 • **Learning Whiteness** 85

Chapter 10 • **Working in Whiteness** 97

PART FOUR: ADDRESSING WHITE LIBERALISM

Part Four • **Introduction** 123
Chapter 11 • **Progressives** 127
Chapter 12 • **Tears** 135
Chapter 13 • **Repetition** 143
Chapter 14 • **Abandonment** 151
Chapter 15 • **Allyship** 161

PART FIVE: BLACK WOMANHOOD

Part Five • **Introduction** 169
Chapter 16 • **The Patriarchy** 173
Chapter 17 • **The Experience** 187
Chapter 18 • **Thriving** 209
Chapter 19 • **Who Else?: Intersectionality, Allyship, and Solidarity** 223

PART SIX: THE WORK

Part Six • **Introduction** 237
Chapter 20 • **The Lens** 241
Chapter 21 • **Dismantling and Building** 247

PART SEVEN: HOPE

Chapter 22 • **Hope as a Practice** 257
Chapter 23 • **Compassion to Conviction** 265
Chapter 24 • **We Were Built for This** 277
Chapter 25 • **Beauty** 281

ENDNOTES 289
SUGGESTED READING 295
ABOUT THE AUTHOR 299

FOREWORD

At a time when we are experiencing a seismic rise in polarization and hate based on race, gender identity, religion, and sexual orientation, *Breathing Out: Ruminations of a Millennial Black Woman* is real. Whitney Parnell lays out her own journey filled with frustration, pain, and trauma. Her lived experience at the intersection of race and gender as a millennial presents us with a unique perspective, providing a glimpse into the complexity of navigating a society where your core identities have historically been and continue to be marginalized, excluded, and discriminated against. Part of her growing-up years were spent in Latin America and West Africa, giving her a global lens to compare and contrast her experiences in the United States.

A prolific storyteller, she keeps the reader mesmerized with her accounts of oppression and racism starting in her childhood. While these stories are very personal, I was able to relate to most of them as my story too. She tells us how her age has been used against her. She experienced adultification bias as a child, and undermining in her early career instances where she was deemed too young to be credible. She tells us what it was like to be called the N-word for the first time, to be told to straighten her hair for business meetings, and to be a counter-protester in Charlottesville, Virginia, at the "Unite the Right" rally on August 12, 2017. She shares her truth about white liberals, which might be a bitter pill for white readers to take, but such an important account.

As an activist and race equity practitioner, she has trained over 10,000 allies since 2017 and shares her experiences with participants who claim to want to learn to be allies but become defensive (fragile) when the mirror is turned toward them. She also points out those so-called allies who take fair-weather stances—vocal when it is trendy and silent when it seems too risky.

All told, Whitney comes with humility, acknowledging that she is still learning while at the same time not being afraid to boldly speak her truth. She unapologetically tells us that her accounts are primarily about race and her experience being Black, because that is the identity in which she has experienced the most oppression and pain.

Whitney lets the reader know that the book is unfiltered and may make some uncomfortable. In a society where race is becoming an even more taboo subject to discuss, Whitney lays it on the line, and she has the uncanny ability to do it in a spirit of hope that love will ultimately win over hate.

If you are Black or another person of color, you should read *Breathing Out*—and even though I guarantee you will be angry, frustrated, and sad at times, you will also feel affirmed. If you are white, you should read *Breathing Out* because you will learn about the manifestations of racism. I cannot guarantee that you will not feel guilty or ashamed, but I can guarantee that you will learn a great deal about the lived experience of one Black woman who embodies the experiences of so many others.

MARY-FRANCES WINTERS

Founder and CEO, The Winters Group, Inc.

Author of *Black Fatigue: How Racism Erodes the Mind, Body, and Spirit*

INTRODUCTION

Which story should I tell?

Should I tell the story of my family's involuntary relocation to a new neighborhood while I was in high school, just months after moving into a new house? People had been leaving piles of manure outside of our door and nails in our car wheels, making it abundantly clear that they did not want us in the area.

Should I tell the story of my high school experience during history class, where we were assigned a debate about whether US slavery was justified by the economic infrastructure it created for the present day? I vividly remember my shock and hurt as the majority of my class sided with the justification of slavery, dismissing with laughter my emotional argument that there was no defending human enslavement.

Should I tell the story of being called the N-word for the first time while boarding my flight for my freshman year of college, after tearfully hugging my parents goodbye? It is worth noting that all three of these incidents occurred during the three years that I lived in Mexico City as a child of the Foreign Service. White supremacy has a global reach.

Should I tell the story of being first stopped by the police for "driving while Black" during my senior year of college while riding with my best friend through a St. Louis suburb? What was intended to be an enjoyable highlight of our last moments before graduating is now a tarnished memory.

Should I tell the story from earlier in my career, when a former boss was informed by a coworker about my "attitude" in a meeting? She took it upon herself to approach and "coach" me based on what she had heard from her fellow white friend about my supposed "aggressive" behavior. Despite no longer working at the organization, she deemed the secondhand concern about my attitude to be so critical, that she returned to the office to pull me aside and share this feedback.

Should I tell the numerous stories from all my supervisory roles, including the nonprofit that I founded and led, when white women under my management would frequently resort to running to other leadership members in tears after receiving my constructive feedback, labeling me as "mean"?

Should I tell the countless stories of how, as the founder and CEO of a nonprofit that trains racial justice allyship, I have been cussed out by grown C-suite executives when they felt uncomfortable? Or the numerous occasions I have been pressured to provide my labor for free in support of a noble cause when organizations did not want to compensate me for my services?

Should I tell the story about how several organizational teammates left my nonprofit due to discomfort with my activism and involvement in the Movement for Black Lives?

Should I tell the stories of how colleagues urged me not to wear my natural kinky hair "like that" to important meetings?

Should I tell the stories of losing several white friends concerning racial issues? For instance, when I received an email from a former friend expressing disappointment in the status of our relationship because, on one occasion years earlier, I had declined to expend more emotional labor to explain her microaggression.

Should I tell the story of my participation as a counter-protester against the white supremacist "Unite the Right" rally in Charlottesville on August 12, 2017?

These are just a few of my stories from my mere thirty-something years on this earth as a Black woman—each of which reopens wounds upon recollection. They are stories that few people know, some that even loved ones never knew. These are narratives that my private self grapples with sharing. Will they provide more perspective? Will sharing them cause more harm than good? Will they create proximity? Will I find relief in finally releasing them after holding them in for so long? Has the damage already been done, regardless?

I spent three years writing this book and another three years trying to get it published. In fact, the title originally read *Ruminations of a "Young" Black Woman,* but almost a decade later, that no longer applied. The final straw in my publishing journey involved an instance where an agency shared that they were not comfortable pushing for a Critical Race Theory book (which this is not), considering my lack of experience. Another instance involved a publishing consultant who literally questioned my understanding of a word in my title. Yes, I am well acquainted with the word "ruminations." That's when I decided to take this into my own hands, after yet another reminder that I could not afford to passively wait and beg for approval as a Black woman.

Putting my thoughts on paper was both empowering and exhausting. Sometimes I wrote daily, then weekly, and then full months were required to recharge from the emotional labor that accompanied the process. Instead of succumbing to the pressure of perfectly articulating my message to satisfy everyone's expectations, my writing sessions became my sanctuary. Words flowed that I had censored from audiences—or that I had ranted numerous times in circles of other Black women. It was raw and honest, and it felt liberating. As I started capturing these thoughts, I found myself feeling emboldened to express them publicly. People have noted my increased public transparency throughout these years. Writing this book enabled me to embody my full, authentic self out loud, rather than just inwardly.

This book is straight-up and uncomfortable, and many people will not be pleased with its contents. That comes with the territory when speaking about race and all of its intersections. This is neither an educational piece nor a memoir, and, contrary to what that literary agent asserted, it is most certainly not Critical Race Theory (a framework that I support and concur, but of which I am certainly no expert). It is an honest reflection about my experiences and where I am landing in society thus far during my millennial life. It is finally releasing so much of what I have suppressed. It's years of carefully curating my narrative repetitively, after multiple rejections and lost interest post the 2020 Black Lives Matter uprising—and a fresh wave of racial backlash that followed. It is an exhalation of my truth. It represents my vulnerability in a manner that I still worry may be mistaken for self-pity; and my openness, which, as a naturally private person, sometimes makes me want to climb into a hole. It offers a full glimpse of my current thought process, which will certainly deepen and evolve with age. These are ruminations of me, a millennial Black woman who is finally breathing out.

PART 1

MY PHILOSOPHY

CHAPTER 1

MY LIFE

On August 12, 2017, I woke up knowing that I might die that day. It was the wee hours of the morning, and I was about to drive to Charlottesville to oppose the white supremacist "Unite the Right" rally as a counter-protester. Throughout that prior week, signs had become clear that danger was likely. I remember deliberating with a few close friends about whether I should go. I had concluded that people needed to show up to demonstrate that love will always win against hatred, and that liberation will not be intimidated by white supremacy. Even though I did not want to go, I already knew several Black activist friends who had decided to put their bodies on the line for the same principles. It felt important to stand alongside them to demonstrate that we would not be moved. I felt compelled to support the residents of that tiny town, who had adamantly warned officials about the violent threat of the racist gathering. So, there I was at four o'clock in the morning, feeling the most terrifying sense of venturing into the unknown that I had ever experienced.

August 12 turned out to be one of the worst days of my life. Heather Heyer was murdered while marching among the group of counter-protestors, and I pray that her soul has found rest and peace for her ultimate sacrifice as a white ally. Dozens of people were injured, including some of my own friends who were present when the car that killed Heather struck the crowd. A whole community was traumatized and will be scarred forever, yet their resilience and camaraderie still shine brightly.

Charlottesville is marked by history. I still don't talk about much of what I witnessed that day, but I used to share a short narrative at the end of my allyship trainings for primarily white audiences. I talked about how my car of counter-protesters arrived a few hours early, but we could not find the larger group. When we finally contacted them, they told us to meet them at a designated spot in downtown Charlottesville, blocks away from the park where one of the most historic white supremacist demonstrations in contemporary history would take place. I shared how those twenty minutes of waiting for relief to take us to safety were among the most terrifying of my life (until what followed later that day). I talked about how, while standing there in downtown Charlottesville before a white supremacist gathering, I felt palpable fear as the only Black person in plain view. With each passerby, my first internal question was, "Which side are they on?" Were they with those who threatened to kill people who looked like me, or with those who believed that my existence mattered as much as everyone else's? I would recount threatening instances when white men glared at me as they passed by, toting Confederate flags in one hand and rifles in the other. I would talk about breathing sighs of relief at other passersby offering simple comments urging me to stay safe.

At the end of my allyship trainings for primarily white audiences, I talked about how, years after counter-protesting at the "Unite the Right" rally, I still couldn't shake the question, "Which side are people on?" I admit, I'm unsure if this reaction stems from lingering PTSD or gaining further clarity on my position in the world as a Black woman. At the end of the trainings, I implored white people to demonstrate, to the best of their abilities, that Black, Indigenous, and people of color are safe with them. This requires more than just being nice; it demands a life-altering commitment to the cause. Half the time, this narrative went over well—usually when I was giving workshops to people who voluntarily took the training with genuine desires to learn. The other half, I could see white fragility rising, and I was relieved when the training was over because it was apparent that I was not safe with some of those people either.

I am confident that most people are on the side of goodness, justice, and love. I deeply believe that love outweighs hatred. There will always be people who are willing to sacrifice everything for the sake of humanity, knowing that if one of us is threatened, then that is enough of a reason to show up. There will always be people committed to that principle, but whether *enough* people will commit to it is my concern and my intentional practice of hope (which I will expand on later). Thus, my final realization after Charlottesville was that tomorrow is not promised for those in pursuit of justice.

Prior to Charlottesville, my mindset revolved around how to do justice work and avoid all danger. Trust me, I still want to stay safe, unharmed, and alive. I do not seek to be a martyr. I want to live to become three times my current age, strutting my way into elder status. However, my mentality has shifted from avoiding danger at all costs, to understanding that it comes with the territory. There was no escaping the effects of Charlottesville. The hatred and violence that burst through that tiny town demonstrated the realities of our hurting world. I could not "unsee" the horror I had witnessed firsthand, nor unlearn those truths. They were truths that I had already known but kept quiet and hidden. Witnessing those realities in such a brutal form on August 12 compounded the impact of such knowledge.

When I woke up that morning, I had made a choice to drive the two hours south, despite knowing that I could die. As I continue this work years later, it is crystal clear that danger is inevitable. While I simultaneously subscribe to the principle that we should actively pursue and prioritize rest, healing, and joy—especially in racial justice work—the fact remains that our safety and health are threatened and worn away at the protests and in the trainings. Even writing this book opens up a new layer of risk as my truth-telling becomes more public. In the pursuit of liberation and thriving, I am actively facing risk and harm as a Black woman activist. That is my unfortunate truth, and I understood that more clearly after Charlottesville.

CHAPTER 2

MY EVOLUTION

My family frequently reminds me that as a toddler, if someone smiled at me, I always smiled back, regardless of how upset I was at the moment. That is certainly not the case now. Many people have told me that I have changed since doing racial justice work. Sometimes it is expressed in a humorous tone during my more vocal revolutionary rants. Other times, it is expressed in obvious disappointment toward my less positive reflections about the world's current state. Sometimes it is said out of concern. Friends and family members will share that they feel this work has changed me and taken away my joy—that they want my "spark" to return.

I appreciate the intention. I have many loved ones who prioritize my physical and emotional well-being. I am well aware that my deeper dive into anti-racism work affects more than just me, and that dozens of people worry regularly about me. They have reason to worry. This work is incredibly difficult and puts me in positions that I never could have imagined, and that loved ones would never want me to experience. However, they understand that this is my calling and purpose, so they support me in every way that they can. Still, I do not take well to comments about my having changed.

My natural disposition is joyful. I am so grateful to be alive, and to experience this world's wonder in its many forms. As a person of faith, I feel invigorated and humbled by the opportunity to experience God's love through many blessings, including the blessings of people through interpersonal relationships and broader humanity's boundless possibilities. This has not changed, and I hope that it never does. However, I cannot help what I see and experience in the world. After Charlottesville, several people told me that I needed to find my way back or that they missed the "old Whitney." Those comments, in addition to navigating PTSD, motivated my attempts to return to who I had been before August 12. I remember praying specifically for God to erase the pain, and to essentially help me "unsee" that horrible day.

Several months into that process, I asked myself an important question: *How much of myself can I get back, and what is my "new normal"?* This discernment helped reframe my entire approach to healing. To a certain extent, I had been trying to expedite my recovery process for the sake of loved ones. I saw their discomfort as they navigated supporting me. I felt a sense of urgency to heal because I saw that my recovery process was difficult for others. By a certain period, people were over it and thought that I should be over it by then, too. I didn't take it personally. It was a challenging time for me, and an emotionally grueling experience for anyone involved.

While I felt pressure to heal for people around me, I mainly needed it for myself. Trauma is excruciating. Of course, I wanted immediate relief from the nightmares and lack of security in open spaces. I knew that would eventually come with time. However, I could feel the shift in my perspective on the world. My skepticism had heightened, and my self-censorship had diminished. The realities of systemic racism's profound presence today had been reaffirmed yet again, in an extremely brutal and tangible manner. I had an experience that deeply impacted me, and returning to the status quo felt unrealistic and imprudent. It felt wrong to diminish the gravity of Charlottesville's implications by staying the same. It felt misguided to neglect letting the experience inform my insights and my path ahead. There ultimately was no "getting over" Charlottesville—only moving forward.

Over time, I sensed my gradual recovery and healing. Just as I turned that corner, the approaching anniversary reopened wounds and terror, with white supremacists granted permission to march in my area of residence, Washington, DC. The anniversary weekend reinforced the ongoing work ahead, but it did not go nearly as badly as the previous year, thanks to thorough preparation. Local activists, including many of the people who had been in Charlottesville, collaborated with Charlottesville activists to show mutual support and solidarity to our respective cities that weekend.

The year-long impact of the events in Charlottesville, compounded by my experiences as an activist and racial justice trainer in predominantly white spaces, has taught me that I will merely survive through adaptation. Thriving will only come through transformation. Yes, there is an aspect of self-preservation that I want to prioritize in this work. I want the essence of Whitney to remain: my joy, my idealism, my energy, my envisioning, and my passion. Those are the foundations of my character. However, the preservation of my core foundations of self, and the transformation that comes with this work, are not mutually exclusive. Since accepting that I can still preserve Whitney and allow myself to transform with my life's experiences, I have felt freer and more authentic than ever. I no longer feel confined by the binary choice of being positive or negative; rather, I feel multidimensional and whole by allowing myself to navigate the concepts of "both/and" and "in-between" aspects of life. As the revered Maya Angelou once said, "You may not control all the events that happen to you, but you can decide not to be reduced by them."[1]

Society often characterizes Black activists as "angry." This label is not only racist and dangerous, but also limiting and unfair. By quickly assigning the label "angry," people dismiss the valid experiences that warrant outrage. By effect, they are dismissing opportunities to receive our perspectives and consider our suggestions for solutions. So quite frankly, while I may have smiled back as a toddler, I am not obligated to smile and nod as an adult when experiencing wrongdoing. I have the right to speak truth to power, to acknowledge harm, and to be upset about it. This does not make me any less joyful or positive, or any less me—it simply makes me human.

I have decided to let this work transform me as it needs to, unleashing my highest power and my ultimate opportunity to show up in the best possible way. This journey is always changing, deepening, presenting new circumstances with evolving times, and providing opportunities for growth. As I proceed, I am committed to preserving Whitney at her core, while unabashedly embracing and naming the transformation that only deepens my commitment and sharpens my character; for if I cannot embrace personal transformation, how can I expect society to do the same?

CHAPTER 3

MY AGE

"How old are you?" I am frequently asked that question.

I regularly engage with numerous prospective clients regarding allyship and anti-racism. I often observe their surprise when they realize that I, a millennial, will be leading the sessions—especially considering that many of them and their colleagues are older than me.

The surprise about my age has been expressed through blunt comments such as, "Wow, you're young!" or "Oh, you're just a baby!"

Their surprise has also been expressed more subtly with comments like, "You're too young to have been around during this time, but when I was younger, [insert some reason why they believe they have superior knowledge about race]."

Other times, their sentiments are crystal clear in their eyes. That moment when they first meet me, the disappointment is ever so covert, but I see it. It's an expression that seems to question, *"Really? This young girl is supposed to teach me?"* Let me reiterate that all of these varying paternalistic reactions are from white people who entered the space claiming a desire to learn.

First of all, I am in my thirties. I am undoubtedly an adult and have been one for a while (my increasingly aching knees remind me of that every day). However, this persistent questioning of my capability due to my age serves as an important reminder to myself that I, in turn, can and should learn a great deal from generations before, alongside, and after mine. My elders have taught me so much as they provided both wisdom and perspective from experience, just as Generation Z has informed me with their fresh viewpoints and energy; as have my own millennial peers as we navigate the times together. We are never too old to learn nor too young to teach.

I educate others about allyship, which pertains to our obligation to pursue social justice in areas where we hold privilege. Initially, my framework receives generally positive reactions from audiences who are drawn to this work—until I address how they can cause harm despite their good intentions. Once the mirror is turned toward them, their fragility is often unleashed. When I confront someone about their harmful behavior, my age is one of the first factors to be challenged. The same white person who initially acknowledges, "Yes, allyship involves self-work, and I have so much work to do," is the person who will then become emotional and confrontational minutes later when I point out their problematic actions or words. They will deny any wrongdoing and claim to have been doing anti-racism work for longer than I have been alive. This often leads to the introduction of an age component. They dispute my knowledge, and accuse me of disrespect for challenging their opinions. They label me as arrogant for remaining firm in my assertions of the dynamics at play amidst their pushback. They say that I am being "aggressive" and pulling the "race card," to avoid taking personal accountability for their problematic behavior. All of this comes amidst tears, yelling, and cussing from their end, while I stand there absorbing it all. Yet, ironically, I am the one accused of displaying immaturity in the scenario.

My youth is quickly weaponized in moments of tension and confrontation, yet it holds no relevance relative to my experiences of oppression. My age was never a factor when I was held accountable as a grown woman in school—an "adultification bias" that many Black girls encounter, being perceived and treated as overly mature compared to their peers.[2] Similarly, my age is disregarded when I am assumed to be the caretaker in various situations where everyone needs my nurturing, a common expectation placed on many Black women in a world that systemically assigns us the "Mammy" role. My age is overlooked when I am expected to perform three times the labor for less pay, a plight that many Black women encounter in the workplace. My age is disregarded when someone is needed to lead protests, risk arrest, and organize communities—a role often assumed by Black women as the natural hearts and souls of movements. My age is never considered when I am expected to deliver nothing short of excellence and perfection—a standard pressured upon Black women in a world of white supremacy and patriarchy.

I have plenty of thoughts about the state of this world and the path ahead. I also recognize that these thoughts have been shaped by my personal experiences, which evolve as I continue my unique journey. As a millennial, I'm aware that there is much more for me to learn, and there are plenty of people to teach me. I revere our elders and am honored to receive any amount of wisdom that they are willing to share. Finally, I have navigated life at the intersection of being Black and female, accumulating over thirty years of experience in those combined identities. Throughout my life, I have also intentionally focused on pursuing justice, and deepened my knowledge around liberation and frameworks for social change.

The combination of these experiences creates a duality. On one hand, my knowledge can only deepen through ongoing work and absorbing knowledge from my elders, peers, and younger generations. I am excited by the prospect of this unlimited growth journey because there is always more to learn from history, institutions, and people. Simultaneously, I have allowed myself to recognize that some of my current knowledge is valuable and well-informed.

I will dive into these concepts more in the book, but I want to introduce them early to name two truths up-front: 1) I am a millennial who is still learning, and 2) I also have insights worth sharing. While I hope that my perspective is respected and considered, I recognize that I operate from a specific philosophy. Not everyone will agree with some, most, or all of it. It is difficult to fully align with everything presented, no matter the person or the position. This is where the "both/and" framework becomes liberating. People can take what resonates and works for them, and leave the rest. Regardless of the extent of (dis)agreement, I hope readers can accept my full self as a millennial Black woman, which includes the both/and of being a positive idealist and a truth-telling activist striving to convey my thoughts and feelings authentically.

PART 2

YES, WE ARE CENTERING RACE

PART TWO: INTRODUCTION

During my anti-racism trainings, white participants often interrupt me with statements such as, "But what about…?" Then they typically mention gender, class, or ethno-religion. They proceed to launch into long monologues about their own hardships, emphasizing that there are many social justice issues in the world besides race; and then advocate against solely focusing on race. Mind you, these discussions occur during race-focused trainings that I was hired to teach—which are specifically designed around this topic. The subject was clear from the outset.

Many white people have a hard time centering race, and especially centering Black people. This tendency is the result of deeply ingrained systemic bias. Society is conditioned to prioritize white people, white feelings, and white success above all else. Thus, many cannot handle the notion of being de-centered, or worse, being held accountable for driving and upholding harm.

I have spent so much of my life dissecting and understanding whiteness. I have had to understand how to survive whiteness, how to be successful in a society that is rooted in white dominant culture, and how to prioritize white comfort and security above all else. I have spent the brunt of my career studying white supremacy as a historical construct, and understanding all of the ways that it is strategically threaded into the fabric of society. I will spend the rest of my life committed to dismantling white supremacy, unlearning my own systematization, and contributing to building a truly liberated world in which all of humanity can thrive.

I was deeply inspired by Ijeoma Oluo's book, *So You Want to Talk About Race*, where she unapologetically centered race as the main focus. Similarly, I will primarily focus on race because I want to, first of all. Race has significantly shaped my life, and my lived experiences were the driving force behind my decision to write this book. I will also primarily center the topic of race because we *all* must. Race is at the core of institutionalized injustice. It is the central issue that impacts every significant aspect of lived experiences, such as health, education, housing, income, and wealth (with the latter two being starkly different matters).[3] Race also causes the most pronounced disparities. As an example, the recent COVID-19 pandemic literally impacted everybody (whether they realized it or not), yet infected and killed Black, Brown, and Indigenous people at much higher rates.[4]

Additionally, race is often neglected when we address other issues. Consequently, Black, Indigenous, and people of color who experience other social justice issues often have unmet needs when these matters are not considered and addressed through a critical race lens. This is why feminism can be the hottest of messes, as it often only addresses white women's needs, resulting in a lack of inclusivity. Lastly, extensive data indicates that because race is literally embedded in every aspect of society, developing and applying strategies to address racism in its fullness enables us to holistically address all forms of injustice.[5] Hence, centering race allows us to utilize the most effective tools to work toward everyone's liberation.

All of that underscores the importance of having trainings, books, articles, presentations, and personal testimonies that center race. It is also why I will be centering race in this book. This emphasis is not exclusionary; rather, I believe that it is the most inclusive approach that I could take.

CHAPTER 4

THE TRUTH

Since Donald Trump's first presidential election in 2016, with each overtly racist hate crime, enacted law (or abandoned one), or act so heartless that humanity has seemingly lost any priority, I have often heard a white person say, "This isn't who we are." As I finalize this book, Trump recently won his campaign for re-election in 2024, amidst multiple criminal cases, a recent conviction, and continued outright racist commentary and egregious behavior. Mere months into his second term, the cruelty, inequity, and attempts to hoard and enact all power are even more deliberate and destructive. Furthermore, his victory against Kamala Harris, the country's first Black and Asian woman nominee for a major party ticket, demonstrated a significant portion of society's preference for white supremacy and patriarchy—and their overwhelmingly clear misogynoir and rejection of a vastly more qualified, capable, and mature way of leadership. Trump's continued support highlights a troubling reality, as the contrast between our proclaimed values and our actions becomes more apparent.

I know that white people mean well with their comments about who we are, but I wince for two reasons. First, because they are mistaken. This country was founded on the basis of stealing land from Indigenous people through means of brutality and intentional genocide, followed by stealing Black bodies to enhance its value through arduous labor and inhumane treatment, and subsequent efforts to restrict people of color from entering and accessing the opportunities and power established by white people. It is a tough pill to swallow, but it is the truth. This does not mean that there are not characteristics and values to celebrate. There certainly are plenty. However, the positive aspects of this country's history do not erase its foundation rooted in white supremacy, and we have been grappling with its repercussions ever since—in part because of this lack of full acknowledgment.

Considering the uniqueness of US history, I will refer to the global majority as "BIPOC," to recognize the nuances of *Black, Indigenous,* and *people of color* relative to the current dynamic of white supremacy in the country. The term recognizes the complex layers experienced by all non-white people, while establishing that there are unique prongs of oppression for Black and Indigenous people that fall within this collective term. This oppression stems from historical injustices that are still the "bedrocks" of the entire construct of race.[6]

I also wince at the "This isn't who we are" comment because I am determining whether it will be worth it to pull at that thread and challenge their desperate notions of purity and moral righteousness. I am considering whether I should tell them that this foundation is deeply ingrained in the United States, and perpetuated by a systemic energy that naturally upholds these institutions. I am wondering if simply stating this fact will be enough to send them down their respective independent learning journeys, or if they will require a detailed historical breakdown illustrating how the system has been implemented throughout history—from wealth distribution, housing disparities, and land ownership; to education inequities, healthcare discrepancies, employment biases, and the heavily flawed criminal "legal" system (which is far from just). Just to name a few. I am asking myself if they will even consider this perspective, or if I will have to face their wrath and defensiveness at the mere notion of disagreement. And their tears. Oh, the many, many tears…

I want to emphasize that racism is not all or only what makes up the United States as a nation, and certainly not as a society. There is a multitude of historical milestones to celebrate, and inspirational aspirations that are also woven into the country's founding. I would also positively assert that most people deeply value those uplifting founding principles, and desire them for the nation. However, I would also argue that certain aspects of those aspirations have not yet been realized. In fact, I would insist that a large reason for that lack of full aspirational achievement is due to much of society's inability to reckon with the depths of the United States' racist and unjust past. Only in doing so can we work more thoroughly to achieve this aspirational, more perfect union that the majority of us desire (which Adam Russell Taylor thoughtfully outlines in his book, *A More Perfect Union: A New Vision for Building the Beloved Community*).

Many white people seem conditioned to believe that the word "racist" is the most terrible personal label due to its perceived implications about character. This explains why so many white people seem more afraid of the label than of perpetuating racist actions. I cannot count the number of times that white people have erupted after I addressed their harmful behavior.

"My best friend is Black!" Well, bless your friend for their grace and patience.

"I have been doing this work for years!" Well, clearly, there is still much more self-work to be done.

"I don't have a racist bone in my body!" Well, that's because bones aren't racist; I'm referring to your mindset and actions.

"I listen exclusively to NPR!" Um, okay? Yes, I have literally been told this. I can't make this stuff up.

These reactions are flooded with intense emotion, leading me to question whether it's even worth it to raise the issue. If we could be less afraid of being called the "ist," "ic," or "ism," we would make much more progress. We could actually get to the work of identifying the systems in which we participate (often unconsciously), and focus on unlearning those behaviors.

As a nondisabled person, I want to show up in a manner that is inclusive and accessible to disabled people and people with disabilities. I try to be intentional about assessing and ensuring accessibility in my spaces. However, the reality is that we live in a deeply ableist society. Institutionally, most spaces are built from the perspective of nondisabled people and often unconsciously overlook accessible features. While they do not intend to be exclusive, they often do not think about it because it is not their lived experience and, thus, not their priority. Therefore, the world continues to be ableist.

I often find myself guilty of ableism despite my best intentions, making me complicit. While I don't want to be ableist, my habitual way of navigating the world without intentionally considering the experiences of disabled individuals means that I contribute to the system. Sometimes, I actively contribute to this system by failing to implement accessible components in my own spaces. Other times, my complicity lies in not even recognizing the inaccessibility when I enter other spaces.

Does that mean that I am a bad person? No. Does that mean that I am intentionally trying to drive continued inaccessibility for our disabled siblings? No. But does it mean that despite my intentions, I still carry the responsibility to identify and change my contributions to the problem? Yes. Only when I am willing to acknowledge my participation through privilege can I begin to transition from being a part of the problem through my complicity, to working toward justice. It will always take work.

Similar logic applies to white people regarding race. It is important to recognize the various dynamics at play, but I also refuse to engage in the oppression Olympics. As a straight, cisgender, nondisabled Christian, I acknowledge the privilege of these identities. These privileges require my best efforts to exercise active allyship every day in solidarity with siblings in marginalized identities and communities that I do not have or belong to. However, as a Black woman, I must emphasize that race is different. Race. Is. Different.

Given the history of this country, where racism was intricately, and even artfully, woven in as a system that plays out through society on every level, we must acknowledge that white supremacy is a powerful energy. This land may be globally labeled as the United States of America today, but we cannot deny that it was stolen from Indigenous people through brutal genocide and intentional erasure. That disregard toward our Native siblings continues through settler colonialism, which is still leveraged to justify the perpetual theft, extraction, invisibility, and cultural disrespect today. Slavery may be abolished, but we cannot deny that it set a precedent of systemically viewing and treating Black people as inferior and dangerous beings who could be stolen, monitored, murdered, and exploited. Immigration laws, though technically open to all, were historically designed to favor white individuals. By effect, many people often implicitly believe that people of color in the country are foreigners by default. We see how such historic "othering" wields its power and harm in present form toward Black, Indigenous, Brown, Pacific Islander, Asian, Southwest Asian, North African, Arab, Middle Eastern, biracial, and multiracial people.

History inaccurately and unjustly established white superiority, permitting white people to construct and drive whatever benefited them, regardless of the impacts on BIPOC people. This cannot be denied. Sure, many white people may believe that all races deserve equal treatment, but that does not mean that they do not benefit from white privilege. Sure, many white people may try to treat BIPOC people well on an individual basis, but that does not mean that their implicit biases don't impact who they perceive as aggressive, dangerous, and less qualified. Sure, many present-day white people now condemn slavery, but that does not mean that if they lived during the time of slavery, they would not have owned enslaved people or agreed to being served by them in some social settings; or that the wealth that many white people have today may be direct results of what enslaved labor yielded their families in previous generations. These are tough pills to swallow, but it is easy to look back and condemn past society as if we would absolutely counter the status quo—as if we would not have easily been consumed by the systemic energy of the times. And sure, slavery may be over, but that does not mean that its lingering effects are not still felt. Nikole Hannah-Jones's *1619 Project* resources brilliantly and thoroughly outline the many ways that anti-Blackness was institutionally embedded throughout US history.

We must acknowledge critical truths to be best equipped to build the just society that most of us want. Doctors cannot heal patients if they focus on the wrong body parts, or fail to address root causes. Similarly, we must look beyond surface symptoms to identify the systemic virus of white supremacy by acknowledging that this is part of our societal makeup. What would it look like for us to address white supremacy like we would want doctors to address and heal our bodies? What if we started from the premise that this is who we are? That white supremacy started as an institutional virus that progressed into a full-blown infection. What if we worked up, all around, and through from that basis, addressing the virus, the infection, and the subsequent symptoms throughout the process? By working comprehensively from this premise, we can begin to heal our collective body.

Viruses spread, causing harm and even death. When we are in a virus's presence, we are susceptible to the illness and must do everything that we can to avoid catching it. If we have already caught it, then we do everything we can to heal instead of letting our bodies become more infected. When we are infected, the recovery process requires intention—medicine, rest, and time—to heal. When we treat white supremacy like a virus, then we can work toward repair and subsequent thriving. Such healing cannot come without the truth.

CHAPTER 5

THE MORPHING

Several years ago, I facilitated a racial justice movie night series for an organizational partner, during which we watched and discussed Ava DuVernay's film, *Selma*. Watching it again after a few years, I was surprised by the depth of emotion that overwhelmed me. So much so, I questioned whether I could facilitate the conversation directly afterward. I pulled it together and was then automatically struck by the blatantly contrasting reaction upon discussion. While most of the room was visibly and vocally moved, there were drastically different perceptions about the movie's implications.

The co-facilitator and I were the only Black people in the room. The other viewers were white and had eagerly participated in the series with a desire to learn. When I asked for their initial reactions, there were two primary comments:

1. They could not believe that people could be so hateful and racist back then.

2. They could not believe how bad things were back then.

Meanwhile, my co-facilitator and I discussed our dismay that several events in the movie seemed to mirror events that had taken place in recent years, months, and even weeks. For example, the historic act of militarized policing on the Edmund Pettus Bridge immediately reminded me of the Ferguson uprising after Michael Brown Jr.'s murder in 2014. The white supremacist attacks throughout the film that climaxed with James Reeb's death flashed me back to Charlottesville and the tragic loss of Heather Heyer in 2017. The overlying issue of voter suppression echoed what we saw during the 2018 midterm elections just a couple of weeks prior to the movie night. Black people all over the country recounted major barriers to voting, particularly the mass registration suppression in Georgia, amidst Stacey Abrams's growing popularity.

The stark difference in interpretation of the movie between the Black and white people in the room was both glaring and telling. While we all agreed that the treatment of Black people was appalling and that they deserved to have not only equal rights but equity (equality alone will not suffice), the discussion highlighted the fact that white people's experiences are vastly different from those of Black people in many regards relative to race. This causes many of their vantage points, individualized histories, and collective narratives of the past to differ from those of Black people. That conversation underscored how privilege can shape our understanding of injustice. It reminded me that we all learn history and perceived "truths" from different perspectives, and that white people are writing most of the history books. The masses are exposed to a history that is recounted from a viewpoint that is often declared as the standalone truth when, in reality, it can be disturbingly limited and highly revisionist.

I think that one of the most blatant examples of the limited history lens applies to the general presentation of racial "justice" in the United States. It skews positively to drastic measures. Traditional history books teach us that slavery existed, the Civil War freed all Black people, and the civil rights movement took place in the 1950s and 1960s to ensure that Black people had full equality. Racism is often considered a thing of the past that the United States struggled with and eventually overcame. Furthermore, it is presented as a tiny blip of imperfection in an otherwise shining narrative about this country's values and success. My lens is different. Many Black people's lenses are different. Yes, the country has progressed to provide more equality for Black people, but the previously mentioned historic milestones were examples of applying medicine to specific symptoms. The virus is still here.

The virus persists because, despite the *Brown v. Board of Education* ruling in 1954 that declared educational segregation unconstitutional, many schools today are as or more segregated than they were in the past. Wealthier, predominantly white schools have abundant resources that set them up for success, whereas many public schools serving primarily Black and Brown students are often located in low-income areas with minimal resources. Furthermore, we cannot ignore the deliberate intent behind drawing school district lines to achieve these disparities.[7]

The virus persists through the enduring effects of redlining, which primarily occurred in the 1960s but continue to drive today's racial wealth gap. This deliberate strategy of limiting Black people's opportunities to build wealth through home ownership created one of the biggest driving forces of the present day disparity.[8] White wealth, derived from land stolen from Native people and built upon by enslaved Black people, has been passed down through generations. This wealth multiplies as white individuals enter Black and Brown communities, gentrify them, and displace long-term residents. As a result, homes in Black neighborhoods are devalued, leading to higher mortgage rates and loan interests for Black people. It is a wealth gap that looks like the average Black household owning less than a quarter of the wealth of the average white household. It is a wealth gap that continues to widen over time. And to bring everything around full circle, while redlining was officially outlawed by the Fair Housing Act in 1968, discriminatory housing practices certainly persist today from continued denied housing loans to Black people, to lower appraisal values of the homes that they try to sell.[9]

The virus persists through a policing system whose origins in Southern colonies were rooted in protecting white wealth through "slave patrols,"[10] evolving into the monitoring of Black bodies and white property after slavery emancipation, and then enforcing segregation through Jim Crow laws. While many people believe that policing should now protect and serve everyone, statistics reveal that one in five Black men will be arrested in his lifetime, and Black women are imprisoned at nearly twice the rate of white women.[11] We see how a criminal "legal" system has been leveraged to surveil and capitalize off Black and Brown bodies, exemplified by the "war on drugs" in the 1980s that ripped apart many Black families based on a criminalizing narrative of threat instead of a humanizing public health crisis. The privatization of many prisons has led to a profit-driven system where companies benefit from increased bodies in prisons and detention centers. It is marketed as increased job opportunities for operating institutions that lock humans in cages while criminalizing nonviolent offenses like weed possession and unpaid traffic tickets.[12]

The virus persists through the consistent monitoring of Black people while doing everyday activities and existing in their own spaces. Dozens of "Living while Black" recordings have gone viral of white people who have called the police on Black people who are barbecuing, selling water, waiting for business meetings in coffee shops, staying in Airbnb rentals, conducting real estate sales, and napping in their own college dorms. Black people experience excessive police force at twice the rate of white people, often as a result of these calls.

Incidents where the safety of Black people is threatened while in their own homes are tragically common. This is exemplified by the senseless death of Botham Jean, who was killed by an off-duty police officer in his apartment while eating ice cream in 2018. He was mistaken for an intruder when the officer entered the wrong home. Atatiana Jefferson suffered a similar fate the following year when she was shot and killed in her home while playing video games with her nephew. Both of her parents died shortly afterwards; their deaths are arguably directly associated with the trauma from recently losing their daughter. In 2020, Breonna Taylor was gruesomely killed in her home while sleeping when plainclothes police intruded with a no-knock warrant and riddled her with bullets in a botched raid. In 2024, Sonya Massey was killed by police after calling them for help regarding a possible prowler. Sonya unexpectedly lifting a boiling pot of water indicated a need for mental health support, but it instead resulted in her death by three gunshots from an officer.

I remember hearing white colleagues note how awful it was to see a surge in unwarranted deaths of Black people for just existing, but this was nothing new. There were so many names before these victims, and there have been so many names since. So many names…

These examples highlight just a few symptoms of white supremacy, which persists like an infectious virus. Looping around to my previous reference to Ava DuVernay's work, her most recent 2023 film, *Origin,* may be her most brilliant yet. She masterfully centers Isabel Wilkerson's excellent 2020 book, *Caste.* Wilkerson's research and analysis outline the strategic ways that caste systems have been implemented throughout history and around the world, directly implicating the United States. I truly believe that the movie's minimal attention and recognition are largely due to society's inability to handle its message.

My understanding of white supremacy goes deeper than many white people's due to my lived experiences and my proximity to those who are impacted by it. My understanding is also a result of intentionally pulling at the thread, diving into deeper learning, and listening to my community, peers, elders, and youth. My understanding is due to my willingness to question what I was taught and to consider other lenses—to validate my own lens. This requires intention, work, and a lot of discomfort and acknowledgment of sad realities. I can understand how many white people may not have been aware of this information, but it does not absolve them from a responsibility to learn what they don't know.

Some may think that systemic racism ended with critical historic milestones, but that is false. I am still trying to determine racism's severity relative to history. Is it better? Is it worse? Is it the same? I have debated with myself and others frequently, with my opinion changing based on the particular circumstances. I have landed on the certainty that all are true: some things are absolutely better as I consider what my grandparents and parents endured. Hearing their stories unlocks admiration for their strength and immense gratitude that my ancestors faced and fought hardships for me to be where I am.

But then I think about the wealth gap and how Black and Latine median wealth decreased by 75 percent from 1983 to 2013. As recently as 2017, there were projections suggesting that Black wealth may hit a median of $0 by the year 2053, followed by Latine wealth about 20 years later, while white wealth would continue to steadily increase. While the lead researcher behind this projection, Dedrick Asante-Muhammad, has more recently noted that we are no longer on the path to zero wealth, he still maintains that we are headed toward major poverty that desperately needs intervention.[13] Furthermore, despite the increase in Black and Latine wealth, the racial wealth gap continues to increase alongside it.[14] It's a stark illustration of systemic racism's impact within our capitalist society. This projection is a literal demonstration of how aspects are worsening, especially by the means of money—a key tool and motivation for perpetuating systemic racism.

Lastly, I recall my grandmother's words as she watched the news in her kitchen, lamenting that in her early nineties, she was witnessing the same racism that she saw during her teens and twenties. She recalled my grandfather's encounter with the police, held at gunpoint by officers during a "routine traffic stop" with the family in the car—a narrative that has been echoed by several of my own millennial Black male friends today. She talked about marching to a public office and rallying for justice, and I think about the many protests that I have participated in with the same demands. She described situations where police were called on colleagues for just existing in public spaces, and I think of a similar instance involving my own Brown Latine friends while in a public library in the white-liberal area where

I reside. Things are the same in many ways, just adapted to the times.

This recognition of holding the both, and, and all of progress, regression, stagnation, and transformation is critical if we really want to dismantle these harmful systems. I often experience hostility from people when I push back at their notion that things have improved, where they will cite Dr. Martin Luther King Jr.'s famous statement that the moral arc of history bends toward justice[15] as proof that since a Black activist spoke optimistically in one speech, then I should, too. But if people are going to quote Dr. King, then they need to quote all of him. Specifically, his quote, "Nothing in all the world is more dangerous than sincere ignorance and conscientious stupidity." They should also quote his statement, "Law and order exist for the purpose of establishing justice and when they fail in this purpose they become the dangerously structured dams that block the flow of social progress." They need to remember that he said, "No, no, we are not satisfied, and we will not be satisfied until justice rolls down like waters, and righteousness like a mighty stream."[16]

Dr. King may have dedicated and lost his life toward a hope of seeing change, but he recognized that there would be much more work to do beyond his lifetime. He recognized that if we did not do that work, we would not achieve the world for which he strived. He understood that we had to acknowledge societal problems with truth and clarity if we wanted to build the ideal world of equality and equity. Thus, we must honestly recognize that racism is alive and well. It may have morphed, but we cannot avoid its existence. I am certainly hopeful because history has shown us that positive change is possible, and there is immense potential ahead. However, achieving such change requires active engagement and certainly will not happen passively, nor with our heads in the sand, or worse, through fervent denial.

This is why I detest the common declaration, "I don't see color." People usually say it to imply that they treat all people equally, without race ever being a factor. I always say that there is nothing wrong with seeing color; it is treating people of all different skin tones well that we have trouble with. Many Generation X-ers will speak of how, in the 1990s, many people believed that the solution to racism was colorblindness, with hopes that if we acted like color did not play a role in any of our decisions, then we would effectively end racism. Clearly, that did not work because here we are.

As human beings, implicit bias is real. Dr. Jennifer Eberhardt's book, *Biased*, brilliantly demonstrates through data and expertise that we all have racial bias. We cannot help that people are conditioned to see color if they have eyesight, and that everyone has racial bias, regardless of their vision abilities. Period. Even if it is unconscious, racism has been fundamentally ingrained in our social construct and influenced our psyche. That is why all those people called the police on Black people who were simply living their lives. Their intent was not to be racist, but something in their minds of processing the presence of Blackness told them that there was danger—particularly in (deemed) white spaces. To be clear, some people have weaponized that type of mindset and leveraged that societal racial bias to assert their privilege. [For example, Amy Cooper calling the police to falsely claim that an African American man was threatening her life, for asking her to follow the public park's rules and put her dog on a leash.][17] My point is that we are conditioned to process the world as we absorb it, and humans implicitly process race. The fact that someone must state that they do not see color is proof enough that they are, in fact, seeing color. Furthermore, in doing so, they are taking the wrong approach to justice.

Choosing not to see color is dangerous because we *need* to acknowledge and identify color in order to address racism. Racism is a systemic construct that was created to uphold white supremacy, and it continues to exist and evolve with the times. If we ever want to make change, we must identify what needs changing. We must be able to compare white people's experiences to BIPOC people's experiences in every aspect of society, note the contrast, and apply effective solutions. We cannot do that if we are not willing to acknowledge the contrasts. When white people tell me they do not see color, I take it personally because they are inadvertently stating that they do not see me; or worse, that they do not want to fully see me because it forces introspection and work on their end. Nowadays, my understanding of their intentions goes even deeper. I realize that not only are they stating that they do not want to see me, but that they also do not want to see themselves. They do not want to turn the mirror on themselves to critically evaluate how they have upheld this system, nor begin the self-transformation that would be required of them. Not seeing color is a plainly false ideology and an attempt to exempt oneself from doing the work.

So let's go ahead and address Critical Race Theory (CRT) here because the level to which it has been politicized is truly out of control. All of that context leads to three main points that I would like to emphasize: (1) we must study history from a truthful racial lens in order to understand the present and work toward a better future; (2) doing so is not an attack on white people or the United States, but rather an opportunity for repair and equity; and (3) none of that is CRT, and kids were never learning that in school.

CRT is an intellectual framework and movement that was developed by activists and scholars to examine the intersections of race, society, and law. CRT establishes that racism is not solely interpersonal but is also embedded through institutions (particularly the law).[18] It has historically been taught at a graduate school level, and no one was ever trying to get fifth graders to take those courses, as recent opponents of CRT have asserted. Accurately relaying the role that racism played throughout the times is not CRT. It is history. Witnessing the vitriol and passion with which so many parents actively fought to prevent a false label of CRT in schools, and the lengths to which politicians and states went to ban any teaching about race, demonstrates the points in this section. Many people do not want to tell the truth about race. The degree to which they will politicize these issues to rile up people as if they are somehow in danger is frightening and appalling. What is even more disturbing about this recent CRT outrage is the lengths that people will go to avoid racial truths and shield the next generation from them. That is far more dangerous than any history lesson a student could receive. No matter how hard some people may try to shield, silence, and spin history, it cannot be erased; nor can its veracity be altered. We are seeing heightened and forceful attempts to censor history across institutions beyond schools, but it cannot obliterate truth.

Truth-telling about race is necessary throughout all aspects of life, and it is critical in our educational institutions. The Supreme Court's 2023 decision that colleges and universities can no longer take race into consideration as a specific basis for granting admission is only a more recent example of the false notion of colorblindness and its detrimental effects. Equity does not only involve providing equal opportunities but also actively addressing bias. Detractors of affirmative action claim that it takes away opportunities from others (particularly white people), but the data has consistently and overwhelmingly negated that. In fact, the data shows that white women have benefited most from affirmative action (so I find it awfully suspicious and telling that the Supreme Court decision only removed the racial component of affirmative action).[19]

Considering race when it comes to college admissions and hiring does not exclude anyone. It provides more opportunities for people to be rightfully considered. Many Black people, including myself, have been told by peers in higher education and workplaces that we only received acceptances and roles because of affirmative action. Hello, everyday racism, once again. I know my abilities and my intelligence, and I know that I have been just as worthy of my opportunities as my peers. I also know that, given how bias works, I may have been rejected from opportunities for which I was very qualified. Affirmative action forces institutions to actively counter both their structural biases against people who look like me, and their unconscious biases that favor white people. Affirmative action is not a handout. It is an equitable process that provides an additional method to eliminate bias and broaden opportunities.

Now, DEI (Diversity, Equity, and Inclusion) is more publicly under attack. Systems repackage themselves in a repetitive nature, and this DEI barrage is just a current spotlight within that larger dynamic. To be honest, the criticism, threats, and challenges have been consistent in my line of work behind the scenes, and they are just blazing to the forefront now. DEI seems to be the targeted redirection of the ongoing opposition to anti-racism efforts, following the anti-CRT uproar. In fact, I believe that the more public anti-DEI rejection was strategic, especially after many people realized that the basis of attack on CRT fundamentally made no sense because it was never being taught in primary schools. DEI was a more specific aim because institutions had actual commitments through statements, policies, departments, and employee positions. The attack seems to build on the Supreme Court's 2023 decision on affirmative action, which, although it specifically limited race considerations in college admissions, has been used to undermine them in other institutions as well. Now the current administration has led a more targeted and blatant strike against the important work.

This DEI challenge is not solely from opponents of anti-racism work, or in protective response to their power. Yes, I have seen swift abandonment of the work due to fear of funding repercussions for practicing the values—which is what we are really talking about, here. Values. Yes, I have seen institutions claim that they would continue the work despite "scrubbing their language of DEI"—and I can tell you from experience that while action must accompany the statements and language, removing the public commitment allows even more room for institutions to avoid accountability. But I also saw institutions that pledged commitments to DEI in 2020 back off over the past few years (before Trump's return to presidential power) because it was no longer as popular and the pressure had subsided. Some institutions withdrew from the work (some suddenly, some subtly) when they realized the magnitude of their own inequities. Others faded into the background because, despite believing in the importance of race equity work (which must be at the heart of DEI), they were afraid of backlash amidst the increased public disdain for it—or they were just plain tired of the perpetual effort that is required of the practice. The fact is, the deeper you get in this work, the deeper you must always go. It is infinite.

The reasons for this DEI backlash and abandon are varied, but the grounding points remain for this institutional work that mirror broader general liberation practices:

- Diversity and inclusion are important but do not suffice. Equity must be prioritized and centered for true transformation. You can have plenty of different people represented in numbers (diversity) that genuinely feel like they belong (inclusion), but equity means that all disparities have been eliminated and people-centered policies and practices have been implemented so that everyone can thrive.
- Race must be centered in order to work toward everyone's liberation and benefit. The data continuously indicates that race causes the most disparities, which is why race equity must be prioritized. Furthermore, when race equity is implemented through an intersectional lens, all issues will be addressed by effect.
- This work takes a commitment from everybody involved in order to effectively impact the culture.
- The work will be ongoing and difficult, so wellness and community are critical.

Anti-racism principles apply broadly and aim to get us all free. Heather McGhee's book, *The Sum of Us,* highlights how everyone benefits from racial justice. On a more proximate level, it has been incredibly inspiring to hear the testimonies of organizations committed to long-term race equity work. A white male baby boomer leader of an organization once said, "This has been some of the hardest work of my life and of our organization's lifespan, but it has also been the most transformative in the best way." As part of a Black-led racial justice organization, I can personally attest to the importance of maintaining this work. Nobody and no institution is exempt from this responsibility, even the ones who teach it. Whether you are just beginning, have done it for years, paused, or even backslid for a bit—get started, keep going, or return to it. Some of the hardest work is maintaining it. I have full confidence that even with solely the people who are currently committed—and their ripple effect of influence on others—we can move mountains. Maintaining is the work.

All of this emphasizes my belief that there will be no such thing as a "post-racial" society. Even in the ideal state where we have eliminated all inequality and established complete equity, we will always have to actively protect that new structure and push against the oppressive systemic energy that was deeply ingrained (and adaptable) over the course of centuries. In the past, people saw color as a means to justify and implement white supremacy. We still see color in the present day because we continue to experience the impact of racism. We will need to keep seeing color to do the work, and to protect current and future progress. We must always see color.

CHAPTER 6

THE IRRELEVANCE OF RELATIVITY

I once attended a daylong racial dialogue session as a pre-conference convening, and within the first hour, I knew it would likely be one of those days where white people would say everything that they thought and felt—all their biases and stereotypes—believing it to be a "safe space" for them to share honestly, and expecting BIPOC people's grace and understanding. It would be one of those days where BIPOC people would endure pools of tears from white people, likely when confronting their insensitive comments and incorrect assumptions. It would be one of those days where, at best, white people would leave more informed, but at the expense of BIPOC people's energy and fresh wounds.

A couple of hours into the session, a white woman shared her desired security in order to justify her levels of fear when she passed various types of men while walking down the street at night. As she spoke, I noticed all of the Black people's bodies tense as we braced ourselves for when she would use that as a basis to justify fearing Black men. Sure enough, she said it with full confidence. One of the Black women in attendance was not having it. She shared that she found the white woman's comments hurtful and dangerous because they contributed to the narrative that a Black man's mere presence is wrongfully interpreted as threatening. She also stated that these types of comments historically led to lynching Black men, and are still used today to justify calling the police on Black people for simply existing. The white woman began backtracking, tearfully claiming she did not mean it that way and was just sharing her struggles as a woman. Another Black woman interjected, reminding everyone that the focus of the session was on race, not gender, and highlighting that Black women also experience racism daily. By now, the white woman's tears were flowing, and, per usual, someone stepped in to support her. After telling us not to attack this "poor lady" for her honesty, a white man made a failed attempt to alter the direction of the conversation toward hope.

"But racism is getting better," he said. "At least Black people aren't getting lynched like they used to."

His comment was both irrelevant and infuriating, and it was clear that I wasn't the only person who felt that way as I saw the appalled and exhausted looks on other Black attendees' faces. This man had just put a nail in the coffin, sealing the fact that our conversation had officially gone into the very muck that many of the BIPOC people in the room knew it might. The white facilitator, who was clearly unprepared for this turn, offered way too little and way too late to try to address the conflict by redirecting us into unsubstantial conversation until the much-needed relief of lunch. All of the Black people sat together during that thirty-minute break to process the prior conversation, crack jokes to inject humor into the atmosphere, and to just sit in silent solidarity. All of that was necessary recovery if we were going to endure the rest of the day. When people ask the age-old question, *"Why do all of the Black people sit together in the cafeteria?"* let that experience be one of many examples. Beverly Daniel Tatum's book, *Why Are All the Black Kids Sitting Together in the Cafeteria?* thoroughly expounds on this, and also further demonstrates how racist behavior starts so young that even children understand and seek refuge from it.

I have moved from being annoyed by the "at least" comment, to vocally confronting it whenever the point arises because it completely undermines and invalidates my experiences. Comparisons like "at least" minimize someone's pain, rather than allowing the immense harm to be recognized in isolation. While the intention behind saying "at least" is to imply that situations could be worse, it often asserts that someone should not feel as badly as they do. There is nothing helpful about invalidating a person's pain. There may be relativity to agony, but why does relativity matter when addressing someone's current suffering? If someone is grieving a friend who passed away, would it be helpful to say, "At least you didn't lose a family member"? Or if someone has experienced a miscarriage, would it be helpful to say, "At least you have other children"? If someone was battling a painful illness or disease, would it be helpful to say, "At least it isn't terminal"? The relativity of these examples varies, but if any of these circumstances happened to a colleague, friend, or loved one, my role as a caring individual would be to understand that they were hurting and to validate their pain—not compare it to others' experiences. Its minimalism in comparison to other circumstances is irrelevant.

I have often experienced this "at least" assertion as a weaponized attempt to instill internal guilt for my feelings and absolve the perpetrator of responsibility. Without fail, I hear it most from white people about the Black experience being better now than before. It typically comes in three forms:

1. **History lessons:** This happens when white people share their personal positive analyses of history by focusing on traditional milestones like the Civil War and the civil rights movement. They believe we are post-racial, that racism has been fully addressed by critical institutional laws, and that racism is a thing of the past. Their theory is that "racists" are just "bad apples" who are few and far between. They expect me to be grateful for what's no longer happening. Furthermore, they are quick to note that the whole North fought for Black people's rights in the Civil War, and that plenty of white people marched during the civil rights movement. Their opportunities to highlight "good white people" during the supposed isolated racist periods are never missed.
2. **"I'm not a racist":** This happens when white people backtrack from making insensitive comments by asserting that their actions, implicit biases, or behavior were not as bad as the most egregious racist acts. Character is the most critical aspect of the matter, and they want to make sure that everyone knows that their actions are minimal in comparison to "really bad" racism. Thus, they are not as bad as other "racists." They strategically turn racism into an identity instead of acknowledging their harmful behavior, in order to excuse themselves through semantics.
3. **False equivalency:** This happens when Black people discuss present-day racism and white people interject that they face similar hardships by bringing up their own problems and experiences to divert the conversation away from racism. This can

apply to our lamentations about anti-Black racism in the national news, and to our recounts of harmful personal experiences. It's confusing how white people feel the need to interject their own hardships into conversations about racism, as if just mentioning racism implicates them. In a society that centers white people, it can be difficult for them to remove themselves from discussions and center the experiences of BIPOC people.

There are different and overlapping motivations behind each of these categories, and at least 60 percent of the time, Barack Obama is brought up as primary evidence that we have it better than Black people in the past because "at least" we can become president. White people emphasize that millions of white people voted for President Obama as proof that many white people are not racist. At this point, I want to then direct them to one of my favorite movies, *Get Out* (spoiler alert coming). The white family in that movie voted for Obama twice, yet they were still literally stealing Black bodies and removing their brains for their own financial gains. So, to conclude, one could have voted for Obama and still engage in racist acts.

I am grateful to live in a time when it is a realistic possibility to see a Black person elected as president of the United States—and the first Black and Asian woman as vice president just over a decade later. These historic moments would have only been a fantasy for some of my ancestors, whose most realistic dream at the time was simply to be legally free. I was proud to have the opportunity to cast my first presidential ballot for a Black president, a right I have because my ancestors and elders endured beatings, jail, and death. However, my gratitude for the progress that they pursued does not prevent me from condemning the racism we still experience today. That doesn't mean that the harm

I endure as a Black woman is invalid.

Yes, the ability to vote for a Black man and a Black woman in several presidential elections within my short lifetime indicates that we have made progress, but it is progress relative to oppression that we never should have endured. Freedom, voting, and the ability to operate in society as full human beings should have always been our rights. The opportunity to live abundantly as our full Black selves should be our right. The security to live without the fear that all progress could be stripped away at any moment should be our right. We have been working tirelessly to build a society that allows us what we should have been guaranteed from the beginning.

This leads me to assert that "at least" and "it's all relative" points of view are *irrelevant*. I do not want to hear that racism today is great for Black people relative to racism in the past. That is irrelevant because if we are still experiencing systemic harm, discrimination, and oppression, then there is a problem. Period. At best, I can sometimes accept relativity to remain hopeful and optimistic, and to see proof that justice work makes a difference. However, when it is used to minimize our experiences or suggest that we should not be upset about current racism, I rebuke it.

Consider the example of queer people being able to legally marry in the United States since 2015. Does that mean that they no longer experience homophobia? Does the legal right to marry make it any easier for them to endure the everyday harm of a heteronormative society? Does it mean that they have any less reason to fear harm, discrimination, or judgment from straight, cisgender people? The answer is no. If legalized marriage does not eliminate homophobia and transphobia, then we should be able to agree that queer people are still valid in naming the harm that they experience. I realize that even this example is from my lens as a straight, cisgender person; thus, considering intersectionality (which I will discuss later), the challenges that queer BIPOC people face are complex beyond my own understanding—and also beyond that of a queer white person.

Applying that same logic to racism, are the families of all the unarmed Black people who were killed at the hands of police saying, "Well, at least they weren't enslaved people"? Are the parents of the millions of children fighting for a good education in under-resourced schools saying, "Well, at least my kid is allowed to go to school at all"? Did the people who were unfairly turned away or denied registration at voting booths say, "Well, I shouldn't be upset that I wasn't able to vote because at least I had the opportunity to attempt"?

When I experience another round of microaggressions in the workspace, from being called angry for speaking up, to having my hair touched without permission, to being asked if I know what certain words mean, should I be expected to say, "Well, at least I'm not enslaved?" I dare someone to respond directly to me and tell me that I should. Actually, that has been said to me. Alas...

I am tired of hearing that we should be grateful for mere scraps in the corner instead of a full meal at the dinner table. That ideal scenario is building a whole new table with a menu that we have contributed to establishing. Mary-Frances Winters's book, *Black Fatigue*, helped me process and articulate how the effects of systemic racism on institutional and interpersonal levels are understandably exhausting for Black people. It's even more exhausting when we're told that we should not feel that way.

It is particularly problematic when white people expect gratitude from us about our supposedly less severe experiences with racism, given that their understanding of race is akin to enjoying a full-course meal at the dinner table. It feels significantly misguided and arrogant for them to make such detrimental comments about hardships that they don't truly know. It either makes me want to give them a full breakdown of education to correct them—subjecting me to white rage in response to not being able or ready to receive this retort; or it makes me want to sigh and walk away because I am drained from repeatedly encountering ignorance—knowing the toll on my health that bottling up my emotions will cause.[20]

Instead of saying "at least," I wish white people would listen quietly and try to apply the characteristics of empathy. I wish they could try to imagine what it's like to still feel the symptoms of a virus, even if the symptoms do not seem as severe. I wish they would remember that these symptoms never should have been experienced—an infection that should not exist in the first place. If empathy feels out of reach (which it often is when it comes to race), I encourage them to exercise compassion. Feel compassion for the fact that people are hurting, and that when people are hurting, they don't need to be told that they should not feel pain.

While there is value in offering encouragement and hope in some instances, true support should start with acknowledging someone's pain as valid and being there for them. From there, we can proceed based on the circumstances. In conversations between white people and BIPOC people about race, the term "at least" should be eliminated altogether. I refuse to be told by a white person that I should be grateful for anything about my experience with racism—especially from someone with no basis for comparison.

CHAPTER 7

THE NEUTRALITY

This book is not a history lesson; it's a breakdown of my truth based on my experiences and perceptions of the world. As this chapter on systemic racism in particular draws to a close, it is not a comprehensive historical account, rather my impressions of the present day that are based on historic context. While I haven't recounted extensive data, I hope that I have made a valid enough argument that racism is real, exists today throughout society, and requires action to heal that entire virus (including its symptoms, wounds, and infections). If one can agree with this statement, then I hope they can agree with an additional truth by effect: there is no room for neutrality when it comes to racism.

Racism is real and it is wrong. Anyone who feels that they are not impacted by race—positively or negatively—is mistaken. A white person who feels absolved from addressing racism is incorrect. We are all operating in the system of white supremacy, which is embedded in our societal fabric. This system is not only directly harmful to BIPOC people, but it continues to center, favor, and elevate white people at the expense of BIPOC people. It creates and widens disparities, and limits opportunities for BIPOC people to survive and thrive on the same level as white people. We all exist in this system, and our races and circumstances determine its impacts on us. Thus, we cannot be neutral when it comes to race, and we must acknowledge racism. If white people acknowledge racism, then they must recognize their responsibility to take action against it.

I want to clarify that I am not assigning blame to all white people for creating racism. This tends to be a default defensive reaction whenever I reference white social responsibility (cue the response, "I didn't own enslaved people"). We were all born into a world with established systems that were institutionalized centuries ago. What I am saying is that white people have a responsibility to address racism because they still benefit from white privilege in a world that is rooted in white supremacy. By failing to address it, they uphold a power dynamic that perpetuates disparity and oppression.

I'll outline comparisons of my own privilege later, but for now, I want to re-emphasize that race is different. Race. Is. Different. There is no other form of injustice that compares to this intricate and complex system of racism. While there are intersections and parallels with other driving factors of oppression like money, power, lack of understanding, fear, scarcity mentality, and ego, racism remains in its own category. The history, intention, institutions, and complexity surrounding racism make it uniquely entrenched and pervasive.

I reiterate that there is no room for neutrality for white people when it comes to racism. Thus, neutrality sounds like "I don't see color," because we have already established that humans have racial bias, and we need to acknowledge color to effectively address racism.

Neutrality is a way to avoid the realities of racism, be it intentional or implicit. Statements made during racial conversations that come from neutral mindsets sound like, "White people experience hardships, too." White privilege does not invalidate individual challenges and forms of oppression; it means that a white person hasn't experienced challenges specifically due to their race. It's important to keep the focus on race rather than always diverting attention to center white experiences. For those who argue that affirmative action, welfare, DEI, and education about race are harmful to white people or constitute "reverse racism" instead of the equity that they actually pursue, I hope there are white allies ready and willing to talk them through their misconceptions. From my experience, this feedback is often better received from proximate white allies than from me. Also, "reverse racism" is a false term in its essence. It isn't possible to take centuries of structural racism and do a flip or reverse so that white people systemically experience even remotely similar effects.

Neutrality often sounds like "seeing both sides" of the issue. It's important for white people to understand what drives people's racist actions, as this knowledge gives them an opportunity to engage and influence others. However, the "seeing both sides" comment is often used to falsely justify the racist actions of white people by equating them with the reactions of Black people. This is a dangerous false equivalency.

Neutrality also sounds like, "I don't want to get political." While racism has been politicized and can absolutely be driven by political actions and policies, dismissing discussions about race as political is a tactic that fosters division. Regardless of political views, anyone can be racist or strive to be anti-racist.

Neutrality sounds like, "I want to stay out of drama." This indicates a prioritization of comfort over doing what is right. Hence, choosing comfort over justice can literally be immoral at times, and many people who make this choice directly benefit from white privilege.

Lastly, neutrality sounds like, "I don't want to cause harm." This implies that a white person is more worried about potentially upsetting other white people by addressing their racism, than they are about the harm experienced by BIPOC people due to racism.

Neutrality is not justified under any circumstance for white people because every time they choose not to speak up on a racial issue, they are complicit—and complicity is one of the biggest supporting mechanisms of white supremacy.

This is why I say, "Black Lives Matter" without hesitation. The amount of uproar that has followed the term ever since its inception after George Zimmerman's acquittal for murdering Trayvon Martin carries huge implications. "All lives matter" responses often stem from people feeling personally attacked, given society's focus on white people and whiteness.

At its core, "Black Lives Matter" asserts that Black lives matter, *too*, challenging a world that indicates otherwise. The structural oppression of Black people throughout history, to present day, demonstrates that Black lives do not systemically carry as much value as other lives in society. An affirming statement that explicitly states the value of Black lives is not problematic or racist. It sheds light on the blatant fact that, yes, all lives should matter equally, but Black lives clearly do not. So, how can all lives even matter if Black lives do not? The objection to the use of this term is not only neutrality—it's direct opposition.

Society has a problem with acknowledging and centering Blackness. Throughout history and my own experiences, I have noticed how uncomfortable people feel when simply naming Blackness. This discomfort stems from various factors, including the pervasive nature of anti-Blackness that is a core aspect of white supremacy. Society is structured around a belief in white superiority and Black inferiority. Anti-Blackness was the basis for justifying centuries of enslavement, the creation and enforcement of Jim Crow laws, and public lynchings. Dehumanizing Black people based on skin color perpetuated the contrast that white is right, so Black is bad. If you add "Black" to anything, it often evokes discomfort at best and danger and aggression at worst. Hence, a term that so boldly affirms Blackness at its most basic value is rejected, justified by the false notion of "reverse racism."

Well, I love my Blackness. Despite what we have endured throughout history, we have persevered and maintained a beautiful and distinguished culture, representing strength, creativity, intelligence, energy, community, and joy. Despite the hardships, we continue to rise and push back. Our existence is resistance, and by thriving despite the circumstances, we have gone against everything that this country wanted or expected for us when we were first brought here. The world may not always see our value, but we must recognize our own. The world may not treat us right, but we will always stand up to that. That is why Black Lives Matter, and I will always state it unapologetically and with my whole chest. Black. Lives. Matter.

PART 3

NAVIGATING WHITENESS

PART THREE: INTRODUCTION

Let me tell you what I am not here to talk about:

- The fictional and racist term, "Black on Black crime."
- How some Black people do not believe in systemic racism, and think that all racial barriers have been eliminated.
- What Black people need to do to improve and end racism.
- How societies all over the world have had versions of slavery that had nothing to do with race.
- Solely gender, sexuality, class, disability, (ethno) religion, or any other social justice issue, without incorporating a racial lens.
- Experiences I have had that did not involve race.
- Matters that are unrelated to racism.
- What Black people can do to empower themselves in

> this system. Although I believe that we have power to address and combat racism, that is not the focus of this book.

Instead, I will share my experiences, what I have witnessed and learned as a Black woman, and the impact of systemic racism and its intersections. I'll also note the role that privilege should play in addressing these systems of oppression, and my opinion on the charge of allies. While this is not a book about allyship, I'll weave in many of its concepts.

When discussing these topics, I am often told, *"But you have not experienced a lot of this oppression. Even though they may be examples of systemic racism, who are you to complain about them when you have been so well-off?"*

I recognize that I have plenty of privilege, and have not experienced many of the systemic outcomes that have plighted other Black people. I had a wonderful upbringing, and wanted for nothing. I am incredibly blessed. However, comments that dismiss my perspectives on racism often stem from defensiveness, as white people attempt to create false equivalencies between our privileges despite our different racial identities. They are suggesting that I have no place to critique society due to my privilege, and thus shouldn't be critical of them as individuals.

I also recognize that my experiences as a Black woman differ from those of other Indigenous people and people of color. That is why this book focuses primarily on my Black experience, which can align with and differ from other Black people based on several factors. So, while it is important to address the many complexities, layers, and nuances that impact Black people, this book zeroes in on systemic racism and white supremacy alongside anti-Blackness. While I have not personally experienced all facets of systemic racism that impact my community, they are still my people, and I have every right to address these issues. Moreover, what I *have* experienced still matters.

I am here to discuss anti-Blackness and white supremacy through my lens and everyday encounters, which inevitably means directly addressing the construct of whiteness.

CHAPTER 8

SCARS

Several years ago, I was part of a six-month fellowship for Christian social entrepreneurs. It was meant to help ground us in faith as we drove our missions, provide refuge to recharge from leading our respective organizations, create lasting bonds amongst the cohort members, and, lastly, help us each develop five-minute pitch presentations that would be delivered to a crowd of hundreds of philanthropists as the program's grand finale.

I was excited to be selected for the program. As a one-person organization and a year into business, I looked forward to the community and spiritual growth. I was also encouraged by the potential to raise thousands of dollars for my organization, which often resulted from the pitch presentations.

Over the six-month period, we met three times for several days all over the country. Walking into the room for the first gathering, I breathed a sigh of relief after seeing several fellows who looked like me, representing the diaspora: a Nigerian woman, a Tanzanian woman, and a biracial Black British man. There were also five other people of color: Latine, Palestinian, and Asian. Of the eighteen fellows present, half of us were BIPOC. These seemed like great odds compared to what I was used to in professional and entrepreneurial spaces. I was relieved not to be the only one this time. However, it didn't take long to realize that, despite higher diversity numbers, the fellowship *culture* was lily white.

From the predominantly white staff and mentors, to the very savior-esque motivations of many entrepreneurs, to the worship music and sermons, this fellowship meant navigating whiteness at every turn.

Here's what navigating whiteness looked like for me during this experience:

- Altering my organizational pitch—based on the leadership's suggestions—to appeal to the generous (white) donors.
- Tolerating comments about "saving" poor Black and Brown people.
- Staying relatively quiet and invisible during discussions about justice in faith and entrepreneurship to avoid disruption.
- Closing my eyes to escape during worship because showing my worship style might have provided them entertainment.
- Smiling and nodding at cultural references to feign relatability.
- Being repeatedly referred to as "girl" by peers—whose implicit bias resulted in distasteful attempts at bonding through the use of African American Vernacular

English (AAVE)—and having to ignore it.

- Pasting on a smile in response to backhanded compliments about being "articulate," as if my intelligence was a pleasant surprise.
- Showing only the positive and energetic side of Whitney to avoid earning the angry Black woman label.
- Avoiding challenging things that offended me so that my opinions would not be interpreted only as coming from the angry Black woman.
- Shrinking away because the façade and invisibility seemed better than any repercussions that I could face for showing up as my full self—and being the angry Black woman.

By the second gathering, I had a plan: finalize an excellent pitch to secure donors, and get through the next three days. That was it. I was pleased to see two Black mentors at the second meetup, and I made sure to get some much-needed time with them. One of them, a Black woman program alumna, warned me that I likely would not be securing any donations based on our allyship mission, just as she had not when she participated. I was grateful for her honesty and assistance in managing my idealist hopes with a dose of reality.

During our closing session, the leadership team requested feedback from the fellows and wanted us to feel safe and open with each other. I took a deep breath and spoke honestly about my concerns regarding the philanthropic space, and whether it would be safe for someone like me. I was met with a lot of "feedback" then and afterwards about using a less aggressive tone, avoiding "divisive" language, and not centering race. Apparently, these were the best ways to drive racial reconciliation and set an example as a loving and gentle Black person that others could feel comfortable getting to know. I was shut down. Royally. I could hear the dismissal of my feelings in their responses. I could feel the energy of disapproval in the glares and eye rolls from my cohort, and in the sudden chill oozing from their cold demeanors and turned shoulders.

I also had some positive conversations, such as with the fellowship cofounder—one of the only staff members of color. After most people had left, he took me to lunch before I went to the airport. I shared with him my sense of isolation, and how I felt misunderstood and judged for expressing concerns about anti-Blackness. I explained how my worship experiences were drastically different from the program's culture, and how I felt unable to authentically worship out of fear of being caricatured. I expressed my constant need to make myself small and monitor my language to avoid disruption. I explained that I felt the need to show up as only "happy Whitney," in order to be received as a palatable Black woman. People's reactions to my voiced concerns justified my fear that any other expression would criminalize or demonize me.

He received my concerns well, validating them and candidly acknowledging the organization's shortcomings with racial equity. He was kind, compassionate, and honored my insights and feedback. The day prior, I had expressed to my fellow cohort member and roommate that I was worried about my safety at the final convening and pitch presentation. I had shared some of the challenges and disrespect that I had already experienced in the small cohort, and my worries that they would be multiplied at the larger gathering in a few months. She listened, encouraged me, and promised her support.

I left the second meeting exhausted, but I was confident that I could muster up the strength for the final gathering and that it would all be worth it. At least there was a possibility that I would leave with a much-needed check for my early-stage organization. Despite my wishful thinking, the final gathering was horrible. It occurred weeks after Charlottesville, and I was still very uncomfortable in large crowds. The staff did their best to support me, helping me rewrite my pitch to include my Charlottesville experience, and they even flew in a Black mentor I had connected with earlier in the program as my own personal supporter. Despite their efforts, as I made my way to the stage, I felt the usual nerves of public speaking mixed with deep discomfort and bad intuition in the pit of my stomach. Something was not right.

Our bodies can capture energy from the atmosphere that our minds cannot always decipher, and my gut feeling was accurate. Not even two minutes into the pitch, I knew that I was not going to secure any funding. As I spoke to the crowd of predominantly white people, I saw mixed expressions of disengagement and defensiveness. There was a stark contrast between their reactions to white men talking about their work in Black and Brown neighborhoods, compared to my presentation about effective allyship. In short, people were not feeling me. They were not feeling me all the way to the bank that I didn't go to afterwards to deposit zero funding that our organization received.

Although pitch day confirmed my fears, it did not compare to the dumpster fire that evening at the closeout. Fellows and funders were living it up, alcohol was flowing, and my roommate from all three convenings had met a guy at the event who had seen the pitches. A conversation turned into a race-based discussion between the man and me, after he had made an insensitive comment. He was oozing with racism, and my roommate, who was sitting right there, was mostly silent, except when occasionally advising me to keep the peace. This was despite the racism coming from her man of five hours.

Fortunately, there were some amazing moments of allyship from five or six of my colleagues, all of whom supported me and called out the man's behavior. Two of them, who were white men, sat on either side of me as a physical demonstration of solidarity and protection. To this day, it was one of the best examples of intentional allyship that has been directed toward me in a harmful situation. I am still friends with one of them. He has shared how that experience broadened his awareness, and affirmed my concerns that everyone had brushed off the months prior—including him, admittedly.

Despite my gratitude for the moments of allyship, that evening remains heartbreaking and enraging for me. It was problematic enough that this man held these views and felt comfortable expressing them to me. His racism and toxic masculinity were on full display. When I decided to excuse myself, my roommate exploded, saying that if I really believed in racial reconciliation, I would stay and talk. Mind you, it was one o'clock in the morning, and after enduring this harm for hours as a failed attempt at a teachable moment through dialogue, I was emotionally spent. Next came her tearful rant about how she had dedicated her life to supporting women in Africa, and asked how I could dare to call her a racist. I was shocked to uncover what had been there all along (especially since I hadn't even been directing my concerns toward her), released by a lack of inhibition in defense of a man that she had known for a mere few hours. This woman whom I had trusted with my concerns over the course of months—a supposed friend who previously pledged her support—was now the epitome of my reservations and fears.

The fellowship ended the next morning, and I just wanted to get out of there. There were sober apologies and a secret attempt to briefly discuss the incident, but I was emotionally checked out. In hindsight, I wish I had booked a flight the night prior to avoid the final engagement altogether. The incident from the previous night, combined with the disappointing pitch event and the six-month lead-up, turned the entire experience into a big, terrible sundae with a cherry on top. The fact that I had confronted yet another blatant moment of racism, coupled with my fears being realized, was emotionally damaging.

I had expressed these concerns months prior, based on personal experience and knowledge. Why hadn't anyone listened to me? Why had I only received "constructive" criticism about my tone and "preconceived notions"? Why wasn't I believed? Why wasn't I taken seriously? Most glaringly, why had I endured so much over the course of six months, to no avail? Now that my concerns had become a reality, I wondered if they would have been taken seriously in hindsight. Would they change their approach in the future?

Some white people with whom I have spoken about this experience have suggested that "at least" I learned from it. Their privilege is evident through the assumption that knowledge always justifies pain. If given the choice again, I would not have applied for that program. I could have done without the additional interpersonal and institutional racism reminding me that I didn't fit in and that I will rarely be believed, much less protected. I did not need another scar.

I needed to share my full fellowship experience to illustrate the painful impact of whiteness. That whole experience scarred me, and I have plenty of relatable stories. While skin can thicken and endurance can increase, harm is still damaging. It was not just the actions and words that hurt; it was also the constant pressure to fit the algorithm of what I was conditioned to understand as successful and right (i.e., "white") at the expense of my truth, or face repercussions for showing up authentically.

Furthermore, there is often no choice or behavior that can shield me from anti-Blackness. While navigating whiteness can be learned, it can never exempt me from the inevitable injuries that accompany this body. I had to learn whiteness early, and I continue to face a crossroads with it as I pursue both success and liberation. It is a daily struggle that drains me. It is exhausting and emotionally taxing. The six-month fellowship condensed and magnified these challenges, reflecting the heightened reality of my day-to-day life.

I want to clarify that when I discuss whiteness, I'm critiquing a deliberate construct of oppression, not people who were born with skin classified as white. Whiteness was engineered to mobilize poor people of European descent and get them to choose their skin color as a means to opt into power, wealth, and opportunities over Black and Indigenous people.[21] It was constructed as the reverse to Blackness, literally. This historical context is well documented, so before anyone accuses me of "reverse-racism" (#NotAThing), please understand that I'm scrutinizing a structural system, not people based on skin color. People born with white skin inherit power and privileges that people with darker skin do not. It does not mean that they are exempt from hardships, but their skin color will never systemically cause the same hardships faced by Black people.

Whiteness was designed as a structural form of power accessible to people of European descent, with a few exceptions and tweaks made over time to maintain control. Whiteness established dominance and control, primarily through wealth, ownership of land and people, and voting rights; along with the power to shape cultural norms and definitions of what is "right" based on white perspectives and priorities. Hence, the subjective form of rightness was inextricably tied with whiteness, and it has been ingrained in society.

Is your mind exploding yet? Welcome to my life. I hadn't fully grasped how much I had been influenced and molded by whiteness because that language and context was not in my scope of knowledge. I often reflect on times when something felt so misaligned with my own soul, but I could not put it into words. Simultaneously, I think about how much I was also socialized into whiteness, and that only in my growth and deepening in anti-racism work did I start to unpack and unlearn what had felt natural due to being so deeply conditioned.

I realize that I am still speaking in the abstract. I have talked about this idea of whiteness, but I still haven't defined it. That's because a definition is limiting. Most clarity about whiteness is gained through its execution and effects. My fellowship experience vividly showcased whiteness in action, revealing its rules, expectations, exclusion, and harms. I resonated deeply with Austin Channing Brown's book, *I'm Still Here: Black Dignity in a World Made for Whiteness*, which provided language and synthesis for my own experiences and their broader implications.

I had been navigating whiteness for most of my life, sometimes knowingly and other times without realizing it. I learned its rules, practiced them, and often succeeded. Sometimes, I even upheld whiteness. But I also suffocated, drowned, and got lost in it. Internalizing it caused me to dislike the parts of myself that did not align with it. My unique Blackness was attacked and hidden, but she was not lost. She persevered and is now free and displayed with pride. Yet, she must fight to thrive every day against criminalization, patronization, exploitation, stereotyping, and pressure to conform for acceptance, success, money, power, and relationships. Every time she is punished for showing up authentically. Every time that her labor and care are extracted and perceived as entitled to. My Blackness is constantly battling the norm and supremacy that have been established as whiteness.

CHAPTER 9

LEARNING WHITENESS

As a child of the Foreign Service, I spent my entire upbringing moving between West Africa and Latin America. Growing up outside of the United States, there is much to which I was not directly exposed during my youth about racism's unique art form in the country. My parents made sure my sisters and I were aware of our Black American heritage through educational resources, dinner table discussions, and oral histories. While we got doses of the experience when we visited the United States for annual summer vacations to see family, I will readily admit that my background is different from that of many Black people who grew up in the United States. However, the Black experience is pervasive, no matter where one is in the world.

My upbringing exposed me to the globalism of white supremacy. European colonizing tactics shaped history worldwide, and I still grapple with that intentional pursuit and implementation of power. Similar tactics of imperialism have been adopted by the United

States, as we consider the force by which the country often makes its presence and power known internationally. The dominance aspect of colonization marks history, and as I unpack my childhood between Latin America and West Africa, I can identify the prominent role that whiteness played in my youth.

I am incredibly grateful for my international upbringing. Growing up around the world affirmed that diversity is beautiful and only makes us better. I am deeply appreciative that my parents immersed us in the cultures of the different countries that we lived in, emphasizing that we respect and learn as visitors rather than imposters. My upbringing exposed me to so much vibrancy, and instilled in me that humanity is dynamic and rich. I believe that some of my strongest senses of community, collectivism, and appreciation for life were influenced by the cultures around me.

Despite this wonderful exposure to various cultures, I was still influenced by whiteness. From elementary school through high school, most of my teachers, principals, and superintendents were white and from the United States. I attended schools that were often historically founded for the children of diplomats and missionaries, and evolved into schools for the elite class, where most students were wealthy citizens of the countries where we lived. Even that has so many implications of white supremacy: that attending schools with US curricula positioned people for success. Complicating dynamics even further, while the wealthier domestic students in West Africa were predominantly Black, most domestic students in the Latin American schools were white. Latin America was colonized by Europe as well, as indicated by the fact that the richest students in Latin American countries that I lived in were often white.

Having primarily white teachers throughout my formative years of school inevitably impacted me. What was unconsciously ingrained in me by the fact that, even while living in Black and Brown countries, I was gaining most of my knowledge and discipline outside of the home from white people? What was that teaching me about power and authority? How might their own implicit biases have influenced what they taught, how they taught, and the lens through which they taught? For instance, would a Black history teacher ever have assigned a debate on the value of US slavery from an objective lens, as my white history teacher had instructed? There is nothing objective about the stealing, exploiting, beating, raping, and killing of Black bodies. Yet, I was ridiculed and chastised by classmates for being too emotional, angry, and biased as the only Black person in the class—and in the entire high school at the time.

That slavery debate took place during my first few months living in Mexico City. I would graduate from that high school three years later, practically sprinting out the door. Mexico City was my first conscious, direct, and prolonged experience with anti-Blackness. As I mentioned in the introduction, my family had to move from one house to another due to hate crimes. Piles of manure were repeatedly left on our property, and nails were put in our car wheels several times. During commutes to work with my dad for my high school summer internship at the embassy, I distinctly recall buses refusing to stop for us on several occasions. One time, the bus driver slammed the door on us as we tried to enter behind a group of riders. My dad shook his head and sighed, gave me an affirming pat on the shoulder, and said we would wait for another bus. Unfortunately, these experiences were not foreign to him.

My mom would regularly speak about being followed and monitored by security guards during her weekly grocery store shopping trips. I now share her hurt and frustration when recounting my own similar experiences shopping while Black as an adult. Still, every week she held her head high, knowing the discrimination that might be coming her way, just as my dad continued catching the bus. This was nothing new for them. My parents have lived in their Black bodies much longer than I have, and I am grateful for the examples of strength, perseverance, and confidence that they demonstrated to their four Black daughters.

The blatant discrimination happened, and the more subtle anti-Blackness awaited me as the only Black student in the whole high school that first year in tenth grade. By my senior year, there were a handful of us, as my sister followed two years behind me, and a few additional Black young ladies attended the school. It was an anti-Blackness that went hand in hand with the whiteness to which I was exposed. It was the stereotyping that came with my basketball skills. Yes, I was good at the sport, and I also knew that I was expected to be good—like all of the Black people that the students had seen on television. Comments in my PE class like, "Of course she's good at this," as I would sink my shots, made me wrestle internally with how fully I should show up to the sport. It was the requests on the school bus for me to rap—an assumption that they thought was justified by the fact that I sang R&B music, as if the two talents were somehow related. And just so that we are clear, I most certainly cannot rap. It was the acute awareness that I was undesirable to my peers, as they constantly asked me to share my blonde friends' romantic availability and not-so-subtly rated the appearances of all the ladies in class. I have never been made to feel as unattractive and unwanted as I was in high school, and those scars of undesirability for my features linger today.

And lastly, it was a sense that due to my minimal enjoyment of high school, I needed to achieve optimal success. I worked hard in high school. I pulled my first all-nighters and cried at B+ grades. My most frequent forms of social activity were study parties with a small group of other students who were in the competitive International Baccalaureate program. I had to get the best grades, do all the extracurricular activities, and rest minimally. I had to be perfect. I had to prove to everyone that I was not the stereotypical Black girl that they saw in the media, and that I would achieve success despite their treatment of me. Whiteness deeply hurt me in high school, and its nuanced exposure outside of the United States ingrained certain behaviors and beliefs that I still carry today. It left scars, and it also instilled knowledge and clarity about my place in the world. Whiteness in a Mexican high school critically shaped me, and it reminded me that anti-Blackness is everywhere.

I first lived in the United States during my college years, where I attended a university in St. Louis, Missouri. Instead of my typical scenario of being the new kid at school, I had the opposite experience by arriving on campus several weeks early to bond with freshmen and upperclassmen from my scholarship program. Coming from the horrors of high school, I was grateful for the automatic community that I was welcomed into as part of a historically Black scholarship program. I found a sense of refuge that I had not experienced in so long from peers who would treat me as their squad, and upperclassmen who let me know that they had my back. Additionally, my older sister was a senior at the same university, and I was well known as her little sister. It was a title that I welcomed under her loving and admirable wings. With all these factors as unique personal precursors on campus, I also saw early that the Black community there was special and intentional.

I appreciated that this small Black community on campus loved me for me, and everything that came with my background. In some ways, I was clearly learning the culture. I had never lived in the country, and that was a different disposition from most of my peers. I was unfamiliar with much of the current music, television shows, and entertainers. I also learned what the term "bougie" meant, which apparently applied to me. It stood for upper-middle-class Black people who had comfortable and expensive tastes. In some cases, I could not fault people for such labeling, but I also wondered if they were self-aware, as we were all spoiled by the amenities of that campus. I also learned what the term "Oreo" meant: Black on the outside, white on the inside. I found that to be offensive because I always identified as a Black lady, and I did not understand how any behavioral traits could dissociate me from my identity. Still, that label came from very few because, all in all, I felt seen, heard, and fiercely protected by my peers.

While I was learning aspects of the culture, I also settled more into myself than I ever had before. I settled into my unique Blackness that was determined by me, and I felt permission to exist in my authenticity because Blackness is not a monolith. I appreciated that I was in community with people who were bonded by our culture, by our experiences, and by our dreams. We had goals and aspirations that did not contradict our Blackness, but empowered it. We rooted for each other, and our connection allowed us to each bring our full selves to a community riddled with authenticity, personality, and energy. We had a table at the lunch spot, which we called "Blavity." It stood for "Black Gravity," and it was the spot where Black people always knew they could go and find community. Somehow, at a table for ten, we could fit fifty and cut all the way up. We would share stories, heated debates, the hottest jams, and comforting shoulders. The term "Blavity" evolved into a brand that became one of the most popular Black millennial digital media companies, inspired and founded by dear friends of mine with whom I remember having many deep and hilarious conversations at that table.

The Black community at my university was beautiful and formative. As I reminisce on all the times within the community, it is easy to forget about its criticality. The Black community was my refuge because, once again, the university was steeped in whiteness. I knew that based on how differently my colleagues and I would often present ourselves in class and with our respective roommates. Many of us had mastered the skill of code-switching because it felt like a necessity in front of our professors and classmates. At times, it meant masking ourselves. Other times, it meant showing certain parts of ourselves. I still often wrestle with which parts of me in public are performative, and which parts are genuine aspects of myself that I bring out in certain spaces.

I noted how I would always leave my room to be with my community, which was often in the suites of the popular Black roommate squads. I know they had to want peace and quiet sometimes, but they rarely got it because they knew that their rooms were the spots to be. They knew they were the refuge locations. Why was it the case that I never felt comfortable bringing friends into my space? My roommates invited their friends over all the time, and I know they would have welcomed me to do the same. Still, my room was for homework, rest, privacy, and certainly not a social life. I would leave for socializing due to fear of being viewed as entertainment, judged as different, or self-censored out of caution in my living space. It said nothing about my roommates, who were sweet and friendly as pie. It all had to do with boundaries that I had created to establish safety, based on experiences and preemptive discretion.

Achieving success in college meant working incredibly hard. Hard work was the baseline expectation. Pre-medical, architecture, and art students were known for pulling regular all-nighters. People would spend days at a time in the library, and would fight for spots between aisles during finals week. Never had I pictured myself fighting for a spot on the cold, hard ground. Work ethics were chastised based on their perceived difficulty levels. The business school, or "B-school," was often referred to as "B-school, pre-school," even though their textbooks looked plenty challenging to me. Then again, I double-majored in English and Spanish, which I was regularly reminded were even less respectable in the rankings.

While I support the notion of hard work, in hindsight, instilling an endurance to work through the night and stress to tears and illness could not have been the way. Yet, how often is that mirrored in society? Success is often determined not by one's work ethic, but also by how much we are willing to sacrifice for our work. Success can equate to personal depletion, often for the bottom line. I think it is telling that the "top schools" often highlight this type of rigor. What does it say about culture that we are reared to give all of ourselves at the expense of our joy, mental health, and physical well-being? What does it mean that we are taught to carry that ethic into our professional lives? I reflect back on how many of my fellow students struggled with mental health. As a residential advisor during my junior and senior years, I had multiple alarming experiences with residents who struggled with anxiety, depression, and thoughts of suicide. They felt so much pressure to get the grades that it altered their entire approach to life. How does that impact eighteen and nineteen-year-olds? What seeds does it plant for the trajectory of how they will approach their careers? How does it impact the careers of those who just cannot sustain themselves at that level—or those who choose not to? It is possible to instill work ethic and purpose in alignment with a balanced and healthy life, and I remember often feeling like the latter came at an expense. And that was coming from little old me, the easy English and Spanish major.

That English major was another glaring reminder of whiteness. I think about my decision to study English Literature, much of which was based on this self-imposed pressure to enter college with a plan. I needed to know what I would be studying before arriving. If I had taken the time to explore classes and identify what interested me before declaring my major, I am positive that I would have double-majored in African American studies and Women, Gender, and Sexuality studies—and maybe even Sociology. Though I can certainly appreciate the value of my actual majors, I know that I would have enjoyed the alternative classes so much more. Instead, I was so committed to having a plan and studying something that would allow me to enhance skills that had already been deemed as strengths—the primary one being writing. As much as I try to encourage others to have no regrets, my life is riddled with them. I am a "what if" kind of lady, and I regret the majors I selected to this day. I'm not criticizing the studies or others who have selected them, but I know that if I had not felt bound by the need to have all the plans for my life at the tender age of eighteen, I could have had an entirely different learning journey.

My college literature journey centered the brilliance of white authors from the United States and Europe, such as Shakespeare. I didn't know that I could study Shakespeare so many times. I intensely studied Shakespeare for seven or eight years through my collective high school and college curricula. I also studied Hemingway, and Twain, and Chaucer, and Woolf, and Austen. Authors like these were established as primary pillars of great literature. My studies centered white people's history, experiences, opinions, and stories. My full English lens was that of white people's perceptions and navigations of the world. Once again, my full scope of knowledge and framing was steeped in whiteness. If I wanted anything different, I needed to seek it out through alternative courses that were outside of the major. Otherwise, the default was white. The African American literature classes had student rosters that were 99 percent Black. I rarely saw white people venture into them because they were not required for the English major. In fact, those African American literature classes allowed credit for my major, but they were courses under the African American Studies major that I wish I had declared. So many regrets…

Upon reflection, I might have enjoyed an English major at a Historically Black College or University (HBCU). Then again, I probably would have studied something more activism-focused at an HBCU. Of the four Parnell sisters, my older sister and I attended the same Primarily White Institution (PWI), and my two younger ones attended an all-women's HBCU. I remember several years ago, my family would often ask if I wished I had attended the HBCU that my younger sisters did. I used to say no, arguing that it was important for me to understand and navigate the "real world" during my college days in order to be prepared for a lifetime of it. My experiences navigating a PWI were certainly consistent with narratives that other Black people shared, such as the accounts by Eternity Martis in her book, *They Said This Would Be Fun*. Now, my family doesn't even frame such discussions as a question. They simply say, "You should have gone to the HBCU," as a clear declaration. They very well may be right.

I don't know what my trajectory would have been at an HBCU, but my college experience is certainly one for which I am incredibly grateful. I learned immensely, made lifelong friendships, and have memories that I will cherish forever. But alongside those positive outcomes, I also learned more about whiteness, which I thought was a necessity. What implications are there in feeling that achieving traditional success aligned, once more, with understanding and navigating whiteness? It implies that white supremacy is real, and Black people must regularly make choices that they think will set them up for relative success, often to their detriment in some other way. My college experience prepared me for a professional life of navigating whiteness, and still, I do wonder about what an intensive four years in a Black institution would have done for me: how it would have felt to have a personal Black mecca for a bit; how it would have impacted me; how it would have impacted my future. I will never know, but I do know that a hint of it would have been great, even if just for a finite number of years.

CHAPTER 10

WORKING IN WHITENESS

I completed two years of full-time volunteer service with an organization directly after graduating college. The experience reiterated the importance of community engagement, and gave me the opportunity to contribute in a collective environment. Such intensive involvement on a local level prompted me to work in the houselessness field afterwards; and even the inaugural program of the nonprofit that I eventually founded was a volunteer-based fellowship that was directly inspired by my service year experience. I built some incredible relationships during my service years, including a dear friend as a teammate. He was the first person I called to cofound my organization three years later, and has consistently been alongside me in support and encouragement. I also met my closest mentor to date, who was in a manager position during my service, and still regularly pours into me on professional, personal, and spiritual levels to this day. As Black men, both of them were also my first examples of having allies in the workspace, and they are real life reminders that allyship is truly possible. I consider those friendships to be some of my most profound relational blessings, and they never would have happened without those years of service.

While working in the houselessness field, I gained deeper knowledge about the issue and am grateful for how much the people who were directly impacted taught me. I experienced the power of being in community with our neighbors who were experiencing houselessness, and saw the importance of centering their expressed needs to inform my actions. Working in houselessness exposed me more directly to a systemic output of racism, and heavily informed my positions about basic human rights that should not have to be earned (housing being one of them). I was entrusted by the organization to hold major leadership positions in my mid-twenties by driving programs, managing volunteers, engaging supporters, and supporting advocacy efforts.

My first five years out of college were transformative and important, and I wouldn't change them. Still, working full-time as a young adult directly exposed me to white supremacy culture as norms that established the "white and wrong" ways to be, a framework and lens that was developed by Tema Okun.[22] It was ingrained in the institutions, and it was upheld through the people and policies. It was pervasive, and it drove the general climates of the organizations in which I worked. It was indicative of the larger society's general operations, and demonstrated that nonprofits are not exempt from embedded systems; rather, nonprofits can be deeply penetrated by white supremacy.

The savior complex in the nonprofit world runs rampant, particularly in organizations that serve primarily Black and Brown communities. During the introductory week of the service year, I met fellow volunteers who shared their motivations.

"I am here to help these poor kids who have no role models and just need someone like me to show them love."

The first time I heard it, my face clearly twisted, and I jolted backwards out of surprise that someone could be that egotistical. By the tenth time that I heard it, my shock had transitioned into an eye roll. By the end of that week, I did everything I could to avoid having the conversation altogether. I stopped asking what brought people to the program, and only asked about their lives prior to the service year so as not to hear specifically about their savior motivations. I could not understand how so many of these white people genuinely believed that they would be responsible for saving children who did not need saving. I was floored that they believed a false narrative that lack of love from home was the sole cause of the educational and economic disparities. I had faith that they would get a rude awakening about their paternalistic views once the organization set them straight during the onboarding process.

I soon came to see that the rude awakening would not be coming from the organization. In fact, the program was the hub of paternalism. The organization consistently espoused all the ways that its programming was responsible for improving community health and children's lives, and it instilled a sense of urgency and personal responsibility in the members about their ability to come and save these children from their current paths.

The organization's mission was layered, part of which was to serve communities, and the other part was to build young leaders through the experience. The participant rules were strict, from timing to dress code, with goals to prepare us for the professional world. There seemed to be only one way to do things, and any straying behavior was labeled as deviant.

I was able to note which service year members were deemed as good and bad based on how they were treated at the organization. As a team leader during my second year, I began to hear those conversations internally. All of it was based on obedience of the rules, work ethic, and minimal conflict. I reflect on how my own reputation bounced back and forth. On one hand, I was applauded for my work ethic, working seventy to eighty hours a week. On the other hand, I was perceived as a troublemaker for consistently challenging the way things were done, particularly when it came to my team's work. My specific team's service had inadvertently become a branch of the development team, planning volunteer days in schools for the organization's corporate funders. These service days often prioritized the desires of the corporate partners' volunteer interests over the host sites' requests. We worked diligently to create alignment between the two and to lead projects that made both parties happy, but it was clear that if a choice had to be made, the corporate partner—the funder and contributor to the bottom line—held priority.

In the houselessness nonprofit, success was dictated by numbers: how many people we supported and how much money we raised. Growth was the main focus. It seemed that if we met our goals, then the next year's goals needed to be even higher, even if we had already pushed ourselves to the furthest possible extent. While I believe in the importance of trying our best, there was something off about the fact that we could never settle into our work. There were always other financial goals that needed to be achieved. The goal was always to grow in terms of people reached, people hired, and dollars raised. Many times, doing more mattered most, even over our quality of work. In fact, I can point to several situations where my work was below average, at best, because we were constantly focused on attaining more—so the quality came second.

There was a constant sense of urgency around our work. From emails and meetings to the programming goals and fundraising, I was always rushing to the next task. In hindsight, it often felt like we were running in circles, trying to achieve goals that could have been reached more calmly. Since that was the culture in these spaces, I would do it too.

Personal opinions, feelings, and insights were confined to a specific place and weren't allowed beyond those boundaries. Everything had to be by the book. There was no room to explore outside of the written guidelines. We had to follow certain protocols with the people we supported in the houselessness nonprofits. There were strict rules about where they needed to be, which were even stricter when they were in distress. I still feel pangs in my stomach when reflecting on some instances where I followed processes that did not sit well because that was what I was supposed to do. The organization was not always human-centered, and the emphasis on objectivity felt like we were choosing rules over people at times. What was in writing held weight over everything else. In all honesty, if I were distressed while in the shoes of those experiencing houselessness, I wouldn't have appreciated some of the organization's decisions on how to support my life. And I must acknowledge that I was directly complicit many times in upholding those rules by carrying out those harmful decisions.

In all of my workplaces, employee value was often solely tied to performance, which was evaluated by several factors. A "good worker" was deemed by their work ethic, quantifiable outputs, and minimal disruption. There was an emphasis on individualism, which felt contrary to the work that we were trying to do. Missions that sought to support others seemed to have inconsistent internal cultures, which often extended little grace toward their employees and demanded a singular way to perform. While navigating this myself, I also noted how it impacted my peers and coworkers. That evaluation showed up in both individualistic standards of whiteness and in the judgment of Blackness.

I saw how exceptionalism was displayed on opposite ends of the spectrum. I saw how, in many ways, I benefited from this label. I often pushed myself to unhealthy limits in pursuit of perfection. I thought that I had to work three times harder and cause as little ruckus as possible. When I was the happy and hardworking Black woman, I thrived professionally. I was the supposed example that working hard and having a good attitude were the keys to success; when in reality, many factors had contributed to my personal trajectory by that point. I had a supportive community of people who had regularly poured into me, connections that provided me with access to opportunities, and resources that allowed me to get by despite the meager stipends and salaries that could not meet an average person's cost of living expenses. Yes, there were some individual efforts that contributed to my success, but there were many other supportive factors that I would be remiss not to acknowledge.

I could see how the focus on individualism applied to me as a nuanced form of Black exceptionalism, which was often subtly messaged as a demonstration that any Black person could achieve success with hard work and a smile. By effect, I could also see the ways that individualism justified a notion of personal responsibility that applied to any challenges that people faced. I could hear that narrative while working in houseless services, as community and even staff members would discuss neighbors who were experiencing houselessness. Somehow, our stated position that everyone deserved roofs over their heads, and our beliefs that systemic racism played a major role in housing disparities, became irrelevant as we discussed how specific people's behaviors attributed to their circumstances.

I could hear that similar narrative as service year members discussed their students, naming the well-behaved ones as angels who were destined for success with the help of their saving hands, and the kids who misbehaved as deviants deserving expulsion. Their original language about every child deserving love and opportunities seemed contrary, as they brashly described these seven-year-olds with "criminal" behavior for disrupting lines and being too loud in classrooms (i.e., for being energetic seven-year-olds acting like kids).

I could hear a similar character narrative within the organization as service year members, themselves, were categorized as exceptional, good, average, or bad. I was unsettled by how "attitude" played a critical role in this type of labeling. The rule-followers who questioned little were raised on pedestals, and somehow their amenable personalities were always tied into the equation. I would regularly hear staff members discuss how certain volunteers were great with their students but were overall problems because of the negative energy that they brought to their teams. Hence, their good work was overshadowed by their deemed negative personalities. I cannot help but note that such behavior often felt tied to characteristics of stereotypical anti-Blackness. Lack of timeliness, loudness, "aggressive" behavior, lack of following order—it was subtle but noticeable. And once again, these conclusions were drawn on individual bases, claiming that everything "wrong" about them was based on their own laziness and poor personalities.

I am well aware that in learning how to successfully navigate whiteness, I often benefited from it as I was subtly deemed as a "good

Black employee." At the same time, I noted how I would veer into the "problematic" category at times, and it was always when I challenged them. I saw how whiteness prioritized minimal disruption, particularly relative to white people's comfort. I remember asking questions about the ways that things were done, and their quick jump to defensiveness by effect. Common responses were, "That's how things have always been done." Sometimes, they would point to something in writing as if its existence on paper justified problematic policies. Other times, they would just shut me down immediately, appalled by the fact that their approaches were being questioned.

I saw how whiteness naturally manifested as power for white men. They would take up all the space in rooms as if it were their right, and people would let them. They would receive and take all the credit for good work while blaming everyone and everything else for the areas that needed improvement. They would tell others what to do as if only they had the correct answers, and they would accept minimal feedback or suggestions in return. Depending on the audience, they would bounce between charm and authority to maintain control, and they would attack or shut down if that control felt lost or threatened. When they felt any form of challenge to their power, they would get loud. They would yell, and that would somehow be acceptable coming from them. They would cut people off to make their points. Actually, they did this anyways, and even more when out of defensiveness. They would fold their arms in a pouting manner, making it clear that they would not budge until they got their way. And that would often work. In fact, it would even be deemed as respectable and an expression of solid leadership. They would "bro" it up and invite other white men into the symbolic club through happy hours, workgroups, and co-meeting facilitation; and they would punish others for any form of challenge by pushing them out of professional settings and informal social gatherings.

As outrageous as this behavior sounds in writing, it was all quite normal in reality. White men could do what they wanted without considering the implications of their behavior because that was all that they knew. That was how society worked.

I learned distinctly about the power of white women's tears from direct experience, and I was grateful for Dr. Yanique Redwood's book, *White Women Cry and Call Me Angry*, which affirmed and clarified their effects. Throughout my upbringing, I had noticed that white women would cry in circumstances where tears seemed out of place. I noted how everything was dropped to center white women as soon as their eyes even welled up. However, I had yet to understand their tears' power.

The power of white tears became clear in the early years of my career, particularly through my experiences with supervising white women. Some days, they would love me when I affirmed their work and supported them (often to the point of literal nurture). But on days when I provided unfavorable feedback or critique, they would burst into tears. One time, I had to literally pause an annual performance review because of an employee's extensive sobbing. After asking what was wrong, she replied that all of the attacks were difficult for her. (There were no attacks. It was actually quite a favorable review.) We put the discussion on hold and returned to it the next day, after she had time to get it together and rehydrate. I did not understand it.

What made white women's tears particularly powerful was noting how the situations would not end at my assessment or instruction. Often, they would go to my supervisor to tearfully complain about me, telling them that I was mean and "aggressive." Many times, I was asked to address the situation or to have the conflict mediated. I was often confused about the need for mediation in response to simple feedback. In a couple of positions, my supervisors saw the tendency and began responding to the women in my favor. They patiently explained that feedback came with the job, and that the women could not skip levels to complain whenever they were not happy with me. However, it took time to gain this type of support from my supervisors. After observing the trend repeatedly, I clarified the dynamic that was happening. I found that I was consistently navigating the process of balancing already challenging work with the compounding effect of defensiveness and tears from my own direct reports.

I had plenty of personal experiences engaging with whiteness, and I also witnessed its external effects. I also saw how it was often taboo to address race. Race was handled very strategically in trainings and external communications, but it was hardly touched internally. Organizations with missions that addressed clear outputs of systemic racism were timid and hesitant to name the role of race within their own institutions. Whenever BIPOC employees raised discomfort about savior-like racial undertones, the organizations would silence them with countless examples of their missions' impact. When employees shared their challenges with being BIPOC in white-dominant workplaces, the organizations would speak to their exemplary demonstrations of employee diversity. There were even times when employees experienced social or professional repercussions for bringing up their race-related concerns. I can also recall several situations where coworkers were suspiciously dismissed from the organizations shortly afterward. Whether it was being shut out of meetings, not receiving invitations to happy hour gatherings, or even being pulled aside by a former supervisor to discuss "aggressive" behavior (as I was), employees who named race were often ignored or punished, depending on the day.

While many instances involving race were avoided and minimized, I also saw some race-related situations become explosive. While in some ways it was brushed under the rug, in other ways the outrage at the mere suggestion of racial undertones was just plain dramatic. People would lose it while recounting years of experiences in which they individually "worked with Black and Brown people." They would take us through entire organizational timelines to prove their active support of Black and Brown communities. They would force us to attend meetings spanning the course of hours to discuss the severity of employees' mere mentions of race. Naming race seemed to individually and institutionally trigger white people at the organizations. They seemed to fight harder to prove their track records of anti-racism than to address the current sources of harm.

I experienced whiteness at work in direct and insidious ways, some of which aligned with what I had navigated in my schooling, but much of which was new to me. It wasn't until I began my intentional journey with race equity that I could put language to these experiences, and clarify their implications.

In our society, whiteness is ingrained in our sense of what is considered right, based on standards created and dictated by white people. This manifests in the intentional maintenance of control over power and culture. We see whiteness through the binary framework of only one right way to do things, once again determined by white people. We see whiteness in the paternalistic sense of knowledge that presents savior behaviors as generosity. We see whiteness in how success is often measured by the bottom line and money. All of this is woven into the very fabric of society, making it difficult to escape without some sense of loss or detriment. Challenging these norms often brings repercussions and is a significant risk.

Having learned whiteness, I also learned how to be successful in it by society's standards. And by default, I often upheld it. I think about the times when I was so stuck on the rules as a team leader during my second service year, that I sometimes lost sight of my team's humanity. I would be so quick to discipline people for being late or not wearing their uniforms correctly because that was just how things went at the organization. Sometimes, I was very aware that I was upholding standards I did not agree with, but I drove them anyways because I felt powerless or did not want to experience repercussions for not enforcing the rules. I think about other times when I didn't even realize that I was upholding white dominant culture. It had become so natural to me that chasing the dollar became my priority, too; that seeking to be the best and at the top was the ultimate goal, and all of it was determined by my work ethic; that perfectionism, albeit impossible, was something for which I needed to strive—and I held others accountable to strive for it as well; that protection of white comfort was of the utmost importance because that was all I ever knew.

I also pushed back at whiteness throughout my earlier career days. I would ask questions about the "why" behind certain policies, and note the savior approach to our programming. I would make decisions about what I would and would not do out of principle, and determine the issues for which I was willing to die on the hill. I would push my supervisors to consider the harm of some of their actions before making them, and I would often let it be known when I strongly disagreed. I challenged plenty and even left an organization earlier than I would have expected when it felt clear that exiting made more sense than trying to change it from the inside. I challenged and disrupted plenty in those early days, and I had no idea how much disruption would be a part of my life's work merely a few years later. The revolution has always been in me, and I attribute that to my ancestors' legacy and what they have genetically passed on to me.

I recognize the both/and of my simultaneous complicity in white supremacy and my constant attempts to disrupt it. It is a tension with which I will constantly have to wrestle, both in my mere existence and in my choices. I often find myself engaging in an exhausting mental loop of trying to evaluate the full impact of whiteness on my own personality. Questions I ask myself regularly are:

- Who would I be if I had not been worn down by whiteness?
- How much has my personality been shaped by whiteness?
- How have my challenges with whiteness sharpened and strengthened me, and provided a capacity for endurance that I would not have been able to unlock without the experience?
- How much has whiteness molded my approach to the world in more implicit ways?
- How much has whiteness shaped my view of success, and how much is that view still being shaped?
- How much of my personality is authentic?
- Are the pieces of me that operate well in whiteness part of my personality, or were they learned?
- Are these pieces of myself okay to keep, or do they need further disruption in order to unlock a more full and liberated me?

As much as these questions exhaust me, I should never stop asking them. That is part of the internal work: examining, evaluating, and unpacking from the inside, out. Doing that regularly informs who I am and who I want to become. It helps me identify areas for growth and challenge, and areas for thriving and peace. It helps me identify what needs to be learned and unlearned, as well as what should stay.

To that point, I want to reiterate that I gained and grew immensely from my service year experience, and my employment at the houselessness nonprofits. In addition to the relationships made and knowledge gained, there were many ways that I was uniquely invested in for skills development, along with grace that I was shown in my personal growth (because there were plenty of instances where I was disrespectful and out of line, myself). I am a proponent of volunteer service years, and think that they are incredible opportunities for internal and external impact, while building lasting relationships and lifelong commitments to the betterment of society. I also appreciate nonprofit organizations' commitments to social missions, the opportunities that they provide to pursue justice through human connection and community proximity, and that they allow employees to gain numerous skill sets.

Service years and nonprofits should be invested in and supported, so that they can continue their important work in communities and society. While they are not perfect (nothing is), both drive transformational work when approached with the commitment to center the people who are impacted, the effort to show up the best that they can, and the humility to continually seek improvement and growth. Ideally, we'll achieve an equitable society where institutions like these aren't needed because everyone is positioned to thrive without systemic barriers or disparities in place; but until then, they are essential (though not the only avenues) to supporting people who are currently affected by them and helping us pursue that long-term goal.

Without question, I am grateful for all of my employment positions alongside my critique and evaluation of whiteness's role within the institutions. That both/and accompanies much of my life, and constantly addressing what has formed me gives me the agency to try to become my best self. I have also witnessed how the very organizations that I once worked for have been on their own racial justice journeys by acknowledging past mistakes, implementing more equitable approaches, and committing to ongoing growth. In fact, we have even collaborated in that equity work together, and grown alongside each other in partnership through the process. So many of us are out here trying to learn, unlearn, be better, heal, and keep moving forward; and it is incredibly motivating and uplifting to do it in community with each other.

Now that I run my organization, the same type of mental wrestling applies. There are still pervasive powers-that-be in the nonprofit industrial complex that often make me feel suppressed, and even helpless at times. Still, I recognize that I have the power to set the tone for the organization's workload, how we will do it, and the climate and culture of what happens inside. I recognize my personal challenges of often aiming for way too much instead of enough being sufficient, and I have to regularly apply self-work and genuine reception to feedback to manage expectations and set reasonable ones for the team's capacity. I play a critical role in driving how we treat our people, and that role should be one that involves listening to what they need while also guiding the organization as a leader. It means finding a balance between working hard and pushing people for a mission that we believe in, and allowing all of our employees to thrive in their gifts and experience joy, support, and rest. It means holding our staff accountable to engage deeply and responsibly in our work, while also showing grace and investing in their leadership and learning journeys. It means finding my balance between being inspirational and motivational, firm and gracious, challenging and kind, and forthright and warm. What seems contrary to current norms must be complementary, and it is not easy. I get plenty wrong, and I need to have a posture that is both self-critical regarding areas for improvement and also open to honest commentary from my team. Additionally, I have seen that significant contributions to climate on a team involve showing regular appreciation and being willing to acknowledge and address my mistakes and shortcomings. Not only is it important for me to do this as the leader, but also to model this behavior so that others within the institution are invited to participate with a similar posture.

While I have certainly recognized my responsibility to prioritize a liberatory work culture, I have also gained clarity that the work is on everyone—not just organizational leaders. I have studied and witnessed the unique ways that white supremacy can show up in staff members, particularly under Black women's leadership; and I have recognized the importance of holding employees accountable because race equity work is their responsibility too. I have seen how this intentional equitable culture can have employees begin their roles with wonder: *"Wow, it's different here. I'm cared about. There's flexibility."* Then they can take a sharp turn to, *"I'm going to do what I want, when I want, as much as I want."* The transition from appreciation to entitlement and exploitation can be swift, and that is also white supremacy culture: this individualistic mindset of take, take, take, for me, me, me, instead of the mutuality of give-and-take, pour-and-receive that the collective posture requires. I have also seen defensiveness in its strongest form in employees who are given feedback for accountability and improvement. They would weaponize equity by claiming that the feedback was antithetical to wellness culture. However, feedback and open communication for accountability are critical components of an equitable culture, and they build the healthiest environments when people can handle them with maturity and work through their challenges.

I have wrestled with determining which parts of these challenges are the systemic growing pains of any organization that is trying to live into liberatory values, and which parts are heightened or unique under my leadership as a Black woman. I am often viewed as the mammy who will take care of everyone, the magical superwoman who will somehow save the organization over and over again when others do not meet their responsibilities, and the angry Black woman whenever I am direct or honest about my experience or employee performance and behavior.[23] I am grateful to another Black woman colleague and friend who so clearly outlined those three institutional challenges for me when discussing Black women's leadership because the language and lens have been paramount to analyzing my consistent experiences.

I have regularly worked myself into the ground, absorbing the rest of the staff's responsibilities so that they could have balance, rest, and resources, while recognizing that such care and consideration were not reciprocated. I have witnessed people perform far worse than they were capable, arguing with entitlement that the "care culture" that we espouse should warrant their lack of effort or inability to successfully meet their reasonable goals. I often question if people would behave the same way if someone of a different identity were in leadership, and I know the answer: no. The ingrained predisposition of Black women being society's mule of constant sacrifice, labor, and care has often seemed to be the implicit expectation of me—even as the organizational leader. Plenty of times, my leadership has been untrusted, criticized, and straight-up ignored because of my identity. Hence, while humility to grow has been critical in my leadership journey, developing and maintaining self-assurance in my knowledge and skill set has also been a must. The both/and of equitably managing my power in the highest positional authority, while dealing with the particular marginalization as a Black woman that consistently seems determined to strip me of that leadership and power, has required constant reflection, work, endurance, and healing that is not for the faint of heart.

This work dynamic can be a whole brain, body, and soul exercise every day, and it is what I spend most of my time unpacking with my race equity and executive coaches. This work reminds me that just as I have my own areas to improve, so does everyone else at the organization. This work means establishing a culture where we are all learning, growing, contributing, challenging, and pouring into each other. This work means constantly having the lens to identify the intricate hand-in-hand dynamic between whiteness and anti-Blackness, thus posing a nuanced and complex challenge for me as a Black woman—leading a racial justice organization, furthermore. The process of trying to establish a liberatory culture has been arduous in itself. We have had to go through seasons of working with, growing together, and even dismissing the wrong fits. We have had to tear down and rebuild. In short, it has been a lot. That is the work: a lot.

That work of unlearning and dismantling white supremacy culture and norms, while painful at times, has also been transformative. It has required that I disrupt this notion of impact and progress being solely measured by scale and numbers, by downsizing or eliminating programs and initiatives when recognizing that we had too much work for our staff's capacity. It was an important turning point for me to understand that I should not have to push myself nor this organization so hard, and that in the pursuit of impactful work, I could be the culprit of overworking the team. It has forced me to reckon with my perfectionist tendencies of trying to solve all problems and bring everything to a clean resolution, and to accept the mess and flaws that just come with the journey sometimes. I have realized that the mistakes can lead to the most growth, wisdom, and improvement.

Through the challenges, my consistent commitment to interpersonal communication has forced me to confront discomfort and honor the values of transparency and dialogue. The personal accountability of constant learning and coaching has given me laser-sharp abilities to analyze systems on personal and institutional levels like never before. The ongoing self-reflection and mentorship have made me clearer than ever about who I am and how to show up authentically while leading. The embracement of curiosity has allowed me to seek constant growth and knowledge, and to also unlock boundless innovation and creativity. It allows a posture of wonder about the possibilities of life, as opposed to constantly sitting in the gloom of hopelessness and stagnancy.

The regular navigation between grace and accountability has given me more permission to acknowledge when someone is not ready or equipped to work at the organization, and to part ways as opposed to continuing futile efforts to push through with their entitlement and racism at my own expense. It has also reiterated that people have immense capability to change and grow, but they must make the choice to do so. They can be inspired, taught, and motivated by others, but the actual decision to commit to the self-work of anti-racism, equity, and collectivism ultimately lies with them. I have recognized that it is important to give people room to grow, and I have witnessed powerful transformation in myself and others when the growth journey was humbly embraced. However, reminding myself that I have the right to make tough decisions when people are not willing to change for the better has been liberating, and it has given me clarity amidst their false claims of unfairness when being held accountable.

It has been clarifying to be reminded that all identities have been impacted by white supremacy culture, and that we all have our own internal work to do. I have witnessed how BIPOC people can uphold these harmful norms in our own actions, and must also be held accountable to the standards and values that we are working toward. While we may have different perspectives and experiences with the oppressive construct that enhance our lenses and actions, we are still not exempt from white supremacy's impacts, which can be incredibly problematic in workspaces if we are not actively identifying and addressing our own mindsets and postures. I have experienced the ever-complicated dynamic of some BIPOC people (including Black people) believing that they should be exempt from such accountability under Black women leaders, as if shared identities allow them a pass on responsibility. It does not, and staying firm to that principle as a leader has come with its own unique set of hurt and frustration. I have also embraced the agency of recognizing that if a white person cannot follow my leadership because of where they are in their learning and unlearning journey, then it is not my responsibility to continue trying to bring them along in the workspace—particularly in an anti-racism organization where the ability to follow a Black woman leader is a base-level requirement. I do not need to change who I am for them to be more comfortable, and I do not owe them the grace of endured racism for their growth process. Whiteness does not deserve the grace to continue freely perpetuating anti-Blackness.

Whiteness is invariably intertwined with white supremacy, both historically and in the present day. Whiteness falls into the bucket of white supremacy because it establishes the supposed (only) standard by which we must operate—all of which was created and institutionalized by white people, much of which aims to maintain white power through manners of control, money, and order. All of which deem any other way—especially driven or inspired by Black people—as inferior and wrong. It has established the avenue toward supposed success that all people are expected to follow, and the notion that anything outside of that is flawed and inferior. It has ingrained the notion that assimilation is the way to success for BIPOC people, and that any posture outside of that construct will be a personal hindrance. It robs everyone, including white people, of the opportunity to create, innovate, and self-liberate by deeming that this centuries-old construct is set in stone.

Often, when discussing whiteness in justice-based trainings and spaces, difficult questions arise about its very existence:

- Is it possible to build a world where white is not the only form of right? A world where whiteness is present, but the supremacy piece of it has been dismantled?
- Is it possible to build a world where whiteness is a component of society, and other cultures are incorporated as equally valuable?

- Is it possible to eliminate some of the harmful components of whiteness, and keep the aspects that could work in the inclusive and equitable society that we are trying to build?

The tense part of the discussion comes when we ask some of the toughest questions of them all:

- If the very formation of whiteness was through white supremacy, does all of it need to go? (The construct of whiteness, not people of European descent with white skin.)
- If we consider that whiteness was created as a manner to opt into power, money, ownership, and authority over people, is it impossible to tweak out just those parts of it in pursuit of liberation?

This type of wrestling is necessary. It is uncomfortable, but essential. I believe that much of society does not want racism to exist. They truly desire a world where everyone can thrive as their best selves. However, getting there will take much more than a desire. Getting there will take much more than kindness. I often hear people say that the main component of anti-racism is kindness. I strongly disagree. I want kindness, too, but we will need many other active components to dismantle white supremacy. In fact, I would say that even if everyone in the world officially transitioned to being kind toward each other for the rest of their lives, the brunt of racism would still be here. White supremacy would still be embedded into society's very fabric. Anti-racism will take work. A lot of it. It will require thoroughly studying and acknowledging all parts of history. History, alone, can do a lot. I wonder about the type of shift that would come if even a good portion of white people studied the history of whiteness, and were able to identify that its construct had nothing to do with labeling shades; rather, its purpose was to intentionally establish class and power by avenue of European descent. What revelations would it unearth to realize that people of European descent lost something through this construct of whiteness by being forced to discard their own cultures and heritages for power? What could they gain and restore from learning about these major parts of history?

History got us here, and what we do about that is what will get us free. We are creating history as we know it, while sharing our stories and operating in this current society. Whiteness is a critical part of society's history, and the more that I unpack my life, the more I realize that it has been an integral part of mine. Naming that has been crucial to my liberation, and constantly working to dismantle it will further free me.

PART 4

ADDRESSING WHITE LIBERALISM

PART FOUR: INTRODUCTION

I didn't have a definitive audience while writing this book. I never thought, "I'm going to write this book for [*insert type of person*]." My primary intention was to release my thoughts and feelings, and to allow them to organically take form. I'm guessing that many readers selected this book in support of anti-racism, and I wonder if they were prepared for this type of honesty. It is an honesty that I have given myself permission to fully share in recent years.

In the past, I would sugarcoat my points because I knew that I was navigating minefields of fragility (and I am so grateful to Robin DiAngelo for coining the term and thoroughly describing the behavior).[24] I would say, *"I don't think you are doing this on purpose, but..."* or *"Before I start, I want you to know that I think you are a great person and a great friend,"* or throw in an *"I'm sorry"* before speaking. Once the fragility was released seconds into my shared experience, I would pull back and say, *"I'm sorry if this is hurting your feelings,"* or *"It's okay, though, because I know you're a good person,"* or *"Please don't cry. I'm sorry."* In effect, I was silencing my own voice in response to their tears. I was sparing their accountability at the expense of my own truth. I was preventing their growth at the expense of my well-being.

I became less censored when I decided that my well-being and survival mattered more than white people's defensiveness; when I decided that the truth was more valuable than their misguidedness; and when I decided that dismantling white supremacy mattered more than their comfort. I was also inspired by the growing number of Black women authors who were truth-telling about the significant damage that well-meaning white people could still cause, such as Layla F. Saad's book, *Me and White Supremacy.* Their public honesty strengthened my own courage to do the same.

Getting to this space of transparency has been brutal, and it has come at a cost to my own emotional, psychological, and physical well-being. It has cost me several relationships, too, such as former friends who decided that I had changed, said that I was attacking their characters, or felt that I was not accepting them for who they were. To be frank, I do not ever enjoy the confrontation. It is uncomfortable, stressful, exhausting, and puts me in a perpetual state of trepidation as I wonder how the dialogue will be received. However, I decided that being more transparent about how their words or actions impacted me was ultimately most productive. I was no longer willing to suffer in silence while people continued their microaggressions and complicity in a system that was literally a matter of life and death for Black people. I always used to tell my baby sister that if she did not try, then the best outcome that she could get was a no. If she did try, then she could still get a no, but at least a yes was possible as well. My being more honest and less coddling about white supremacy is my application of this philosophy: I am sharing with the hopes of possible change, and the understanding that everything may stay the same. My being silent and continuing to endure injury ultimately yielded no opportunity for improvement. I am reminding myself of this courageous position and decision as I dive in head-first to discuss white liberalism.

CHAPTER 11

PROGRESSIVES

Several years ago, I worked extensively with a white-liberal church that verbally expressed their deep commitment to anti-racism. I initially thought that the engagement was a great opportunity to partner with an organization that trusted me to help lead this important work. It quickly became an exhausting experience, where I spent the brunt of my time engaging with them on all types of matters. Then it got out of control when I became their "go-to" Black teacher. They sucked the life out of me by expecting my constant availability to facilitate trainings, lead church services, and provide impromptu one-on-one coaching sessions during meetings. Finally, I put my foot down when it became clear that much of my labor was being given and taken for free. Discussions about appropriate compensation quickly became problematic as the church maneuvered ways to pay me far below equitably, and simultaneously profit off my labor.

An example of exploitative profiting was when a training

participant made a check donation to my organization. I had been hired by the church to lead a workshop, and the attendee had been so moved by her learning that she wanted to personally support our mission with her own funds. The church literally asked me to subtract that donation amount from their payment for the training. It was a mess. Similar conversations ended with me stating that I would only provide paid services, which would cease much of the labor and time that I had been regularly giving. I will just wrap up that story by saying that they did not respond well.

I was disappointed by the evolution of this institutional relationship and how my labor was exploited. More than anything, I was disappointed by the people involved, particularly a white person who had been one of my strongest allies in the beginning. He was encouraging, seemed genuinely committed to the work, and played a major role in establishing the partnership at the church. I let my gratitude for his support overshadow his grave errors. I tried to ignore the fact that he was extremely pressed to become a trainer of my material, and that he pushed for his church to partner so that many of their members could become trainers as well. His obsession with having facilitation access to my content seemed to overshadow his desire to implement its principles. I tried to excuse his increasing defensiveness whenever I shared my concerns about his lack of inward work. For example, when I would invite him to reflect on how the content applied to areas where he needed to improve his own behavior, he would dismiss it and say that his main priority was to influence other people to change their behavior. Additionally, when I directly addressed the fact that he had interrupted me several times during a conversation, and that he did that regularly when we were in dialogue, he said that I needed to stop giving him a hard time when he was trying to bring along people who were doing far worse. And when I would express concern that he was putting more energy into finding ways to equip church members to lead my training, instead of directing his energy toward implementing more equitable practices within the institution, he would push back and say that "training the trainer" should be the highest priority. All he cared about was reaching other conservatives, and he frequently shared his stress about getting others to "wake up" by acting and thinking like him.

This person spent a lot of time crying whenever we talked about race, turning the conversations to *his* struggles about the stress of racism—mind you, while talking to me, a Black woman who regularly experienced racism. He shut down when I started standing my ground about compensation, and began avoiding conversations that sought to address the matter. And then he exploded. He yelled and cussed at me as we sat in a group meeting to discuss the partnership moving forward, while the other woman in the meeting cried, shocked and frozen by this reaction from the church's authority figure.

After giving him time to regain his composure, we discussed what happened a few days later over a meal (as I knew that a public restaurant setting would help ensure more measured behavior). He apologized and said, "That was not me." And even though we closed that matter on civil terms, it was clear that the relationship was different. I could not trust a relationship with someone who could be so complicit in my exploitation. I was disappointed by his devolved behavior as things became more difficult. Yet, I was not surprised. While his actions certainly didn't define his entire character as a person, his explosive response to addressing racial dynamics wasn't new for me.

People often assume that Black harm comes solely from less progressive perpetrators. I wonder how many people selected this book assuming that most of the content about racism was referring to a more conservative demographic. If they did, then they were mistaken. Racism does not have a political affiliation, which I can speak to firsthand. Most of my perspective applies just as much to progressive white people as it does to anyone else. Most of my examples of disrespectful interactions are with white liberals. Most of my daily injuries come from white liberals.

My personal calling is not to convince people that racism exists. Trust me, I came to that clarity early in this work. There are some amazingly patient and gracious Black people who have that gift. I do not. Rather, my line of work involves equipping and empowering people to drive change because they know that racism is alive and well. The problem is that the audiences with whom I engage often are not aware or informed of the full problem, and there is much more learning and reflection involved than they expect. This is based on the common narrative that I encounter as people give introductions about their motivations to participate in said trainings.

1. "I'm here to learn how to work on my racist family member."
2. "I'm here because I just don't understand these Trump supporters."
3. "I'm here because it just breaks my heart to see all of these poor (Black) people suffer so much, and I want to help them."

People are hit with the hard reality throughout the course of my trainings that, while influencing other white people is critical to white allyship, turning the mirror on their own complicity and harm is a requirement. I often emphasize that allyship is only effective from the "inside, out." Inner work must be a priority, and that will, in turn, affect their outward actions. Upon driving home this truth, I am sometimes met with people who come with open hearts and minds, and with various political affiliations. By effect, they are incredibly receptive to the material, and identify personal growth and actions to effectively move forward. However, particularly in liberal spaces, I often come across fragility in the forms below, which I have accompanied with what goes through my head in real time:

1. **Denial associated with upbringing:** *"I could not possibly be racist. My parents taught me to love everyone, and I have done a laundry list of good work to show that I couldn't possibly do anything racist."* So, now they are absolved of any possible racism, ever, because they were raised to be nice people.
2. **Claims of attack and victimization:** *"You are attacking me, and it really hurts my feelings that you would lump me into a category that is not in my heart."* Now they are the victims, and this is all about the harm that they face as white people...while we discuss racism.
3. **False comparison to their own marginalized experiences:** *"I deal with sexism every day, so I know exactly what racism feels like. We cannot forget about women, class, and religion. We always focus on race and then forget about the oppression that others of us have gone through."* Now, this race-based training is no longer about race at all.
4. **Criticism that I am turning away good people:** *"I am already on your side. Why are you attacking me? You don't want to lose us when there are bigger problems out there."* Now I am the angry Black woman who needs to do better because I have suggested that they should do better.

5. **Claims to not see color:** *"I cannot be racist because I do not even see color. When I saw you, I just thought, 'What a wonderful person.' I do not even notice that you are Black. I just see you as human."* My frustrations about this inaccuracy have already been shared. Next!
6. **A laundry list of all the ways that they have done anti-racism work:** *"I marched in the sixties, I worked with inner-city kids, I have a Black Lives Matter sign on my front lawn, and I love [insert Black musical artist or show/movie with a predominantly Black cast]."* They often attack my age here, noting that they have been doing anti-racism work for longer than I have been alive.
7. **Claims that their youth makes them optimally aware and flawless by default:** *"My generation already knows these things; I took this class in college, I go to protests all the time, I am constantly calling out my racist parents, and I follow so many Black influencers and activists on social media."* White supremacy is the air we breathe, meaning that young people are just as susceptible to, and impacted by, its influence.
8. **Pushback against my assertions by claiming that they support a different philosophical approach:** *"The civil rights movement was all about nonviolent action, and that really worked. In my experience, I have seen that a less confrontational approach is the best way for you to reach people."* Again, now the work is on me to be the palatable Black person whom they can humanize, and only then can they be expected to do the work. Also, please study the real civil rights movement, which had confrontation and disruption as one of its primary tactics.
9. **Some sort of pushback, invoking Dr. King or Jesus:** *"Dr. King and Jesus were all about love. What you are doing and saying will*

not reach anyone, and it goes against their or my stance of love prevailing." [Insert "I have a dream" quote or Bible verse.] Well, they should check out Dr. King's "Letter from Birmingham Jail," where he talks about the white moderate being Black people's great stumbling block, and then get back to me.[25] Also, Jesus literally flipped tables when witnessing immorality. Truth-telling and love are not mutually exclusive.

10. **Excuses for lack of knowledge and expectations of Black patience:** "*I do not know what I do not know, so it is more helpful if you kindly teach me rather than just attack me. You need to be easier on me because a lot of this is new for me.*" While the information presented in my training may be new for some of the attendees, this would be a great opportunity for them to learn from my speaking truth to power. Again, palatability seems to be the priority. And just so that we are clear, sharing "truth" is not synonymous with "attacking." I do not attack others in my trainings.
11. **Shutting down completely, often with crossed arms and furrowed brows:** "*Well, if I'm such a bad person, then I guess I shouldn't be doing anything anyway. Hmph.*" The immaturity in these spaces is often laughable. Picture an adult in this posture.
12. **Tears, yelling, cussing, and more tears:** "*You are a reverse racist; you are mean; you are wrong; I am an amazing white ally; I have so many Black friends; and I am hurt.*" I cannot.
13. **Coming to the defense of another white person who is crying, yelling, cussing, and crying some more:** "*You should not attack them this way. You are hurting their feelings and being too hard on them. I felt that I had to step in.*" White solidarity over Black harm wins again, and the cycle continues.

14. **Assertive exiting:** *"I did not sign up for this abuse, so I am leaving."* Alright, bye.

Those are just a few standard quotes, which are common enough to be regular subject matters between Black people at cookouts or when recounting the day's narrative over dinner or drinks. All of it is harmful. The more that the thread is pulled, the greater damage we see that white people can have on personal, interpersonal, and institutional levels. All to say, white liberals are not exempt from holding themselves accountable to examine their participation in this system. Thus, even through the few referenced examples, white liberals cannot only be harmful, but dangerous. It is dangerous to deny complicity because that means that its continuation can result in compounded and ongoing detriment. It is dangerous to think that one has reached some sort of quota for their allyship because that wrongfully exempts them from vital continued work. It is dangerous to accuse Black people of wrongdoing when we share honestly, because that can bring repercussions and literal punishment toward Black people in a society that inherently criminalizes us. All of this is so dangerous, yet it continues to be my everyday experience in this line of work. Just about every day, I am witnessing the danger of progressive white people who think that they are the sole solution...and that terrifies me.

CHAPTER 12

TEARS

Every time a white person says or does something problematic, before addressing it, I take half a second to ask myself, "Will this be worth it?" My ability to quickly process the question is a trained skill, given the frequency with which I must ask it. I ask myself that question because I know the potential reaction. Speaking my truth or addressing injury could come at a cost. It could come at the risk of my own emotional labor, and even potential repercussions. History shows us that when white people claim any form of distress, discomfort, anger, or fear, not only do the masses flock toward addressing them first, but they will often retaliate against BIPOC people who were the supposed threats—especially Black people. And quite frankly, all of that aside, sometimes I just do not have the patience to navigate tears when I am already trying to deal with the pain that I just endured. It is just an additional layer of burden that comes with my Blackness.

Thus, with the recognition of every microaggression, subtle action, or well-meaning offense, I ask myself:

1. Will this be worth it?
2. Should I address this?
3. Is this important enough for me to address that I am willing to face the potential backlash?

My response depends on the day. My reaction is circumstantial based on many factors, including my current endurance level, the likelihood of their repeated behavior toward me or someone else, the number of times that I have already experienced this or similar behavior from them, the gravity of the action, and even just my position of principle. Sometimes, I can experience the exact same offense from two different people on separate occasions, and decide to confront it on one day and let it slide on the other. Sometimes, I can receive it several times from the same person and confront it one day, and not the next. Sometimes, the fact that it is a recurring offense from the same person can dissuade me from addressing it because, despite being given the same feedback multiple times, their behavior is not changing, so it is no longer worth my energy. Sometimes, I am aware of the power dynamics involved and do not want to risk potentially losing the job or opportunity, despite the validity of my feelings. Even at the organization that I founded and run, I have gone through the same process, knowing that a white employee's tears could still wreak so much havoc on the work, culture, and my mental health within the confines of the organization because of our regular engagement. There are so many variables involved with the decision to address a situation that I am exhausted before I have even confronted it. Often, what feels like step one for a white person is already step one hundred for the Black person—in just that week.

The deeper that I have gone into anti-racism work, and particularly the more that I have interacted with white progressive people, I find myself asking the "worth it" question more often. That "worth it" question is most pressing with my lack of patience and energy for a particular action over them all: tears. The presence of white tears has exhausted me, enraged me, and numbed me. I find myself navigating white tears so regularly that I have a menu of responses that I would like to say. The Whitney of my dreams would like to say:

1. "Please excuse yourself, clean up, and return when you have gotten it together, because I need you to handle this like an adult."
2. "Stop crying because you are making this about you. You have made this about why you are crying, how you are feeling, and how I should react to your tears, rather than the harm about which I have confronted you."
3. "Stop crying and blaming me for attacking you because now I am viewed as the angry and wrong one for hurting this poor innocent person—even though I am the one who was negatively impacted by your action."
4. "Stop crying because your emotional release increases my emotional labor. Every tear that you shed is compounding the burden that I must carry."
5. "Stop crying because it will not stop me from holding you accountable for your actions. I know you are used to the world stopping when you get upset, but you still must face your responsibilities."
6. "Stop crying because your tears have historically gotten us killed. From lynching to calling the police, when you cry, the world

blames us and will do anything to appease your discomfort—even at the expense of our lives. Your crying is killing us."

I want to say all of this, and sometimes I do. Admittedly, there are still many times when I do not say anything. Believe it or not, I do have empathy and compassion. That may come as a surprise, given the tone of this book. In all honesty, I do not like seeing people in distress. It used to be the case that if someone cried, I would drop everything to support and comfort them. In my earlier days of doing anti-racism work, the same method applied. I would address a white person's racist action, they would start to cry, and then my reaction would be one of the following:

1. "Oh no, what's wrong?" Sometimes that would be a legitimate question because I genuinely could not understand why they were crying.
2. "It's okay, though. Don't worry, what you did wasn't that bad." Even if their action was that bad, I found myself wanting to minimize the impact to relieve their distress.
3. "You're still a good person. We're still friends." Somehow, I was then responsible for encouraging them, even though they had hurt me. And somehow, assuring them that our relationship had not changed despite their actions was critical. In hindsight, sometimes the relationship should have changed because the action was so egregious. For the sake of self-preservation and respect, there were times when new boundaries were justified, but I outwardly maintained the relationship as if all was well. However, the incident made me aware of who they could be, and it was noted.
4. "It's okay to cry. I know it's hard." I understand that crying can be cathartic, and that dealing with concepts and accountability

in new ways can be challenging. I would find myself giving this notion more weight than my own difficulties while experiencing their behavior. When discussing race, white people need to understand that there are times when they just need to hold back their emotions. Quite frankly, hearing about one's racism is not nearly as bad as experiencing racism. So, if I can hold back my warranted tears with every microaggression and racist action, then they can hold back their tears when they are confronted about them.

5. "I'm sorry." I shudder at how often I have apologized to white people for "making" them cry. How I took on the burden of fault due to their mind games, manipulation, and gaslighting. How I internalized my own oppression by blaming myself for being "angry," rather than holding them accountable for making me angry. How I knew that even though I may not have been wrong, stopping their tears to guarantee my safety was much more important than facing repercussions for upsetting white people.

I am different now. Now, I unabashedly incorporate content specifically about tears into my trainings. I share how tears are often the go-to output of fragility, like a gag reflex of defensiveness. I share how tears have depleted my patience because I regularly experience them as a barrier to learning and accountability in this work. I share how tears exhaust me. In addition to the labor involved with addressing their fragility, being expected to comfort white people who are crying out of distress from being overwhelmed by racism's magnitude feels burdensome. I regularly found myself patting white people on their backs and telling them that it would be okay, as they wailed about how stressful racism was for them. Yes, this Black woman was comforting these white people about their stress with racism.

In my trainings I share how crying deepens distrust because Black people have countless examples of tears in response to addressing racist acts, that they often decide it is better not to confront at all. And then, when white people complain that they "don't know what they don't know," I try to help them understand that when Black people try to address that ignorance, the reaction of crying makes us skeptical that white people really want to know or that they have the maturity to handle it. I share how tears are dangerous for us because we have too many examples of being punished, fired, attacked, jailed, and killed based on someone crying about our mere existence or interaction.

I am drowning in white tears every day. And I need air.

I am sure that white people do not mean to cause so much distress when they cry, but it is important to know that they do. I know what it is like to want to cry and to do everything that I can to hold it in, but the tears still escape. Sometimes, we just cannot control them. However, I am asking white people to try to control their emotions and reactions when it comes to race. While I am referring to the literal tears that are so prevalent in this space, I am also speaking to all types of emotional outbursts: yelling, cussing, screaming...I have gotten all of it from educators, nonprofit employees, C-suite corporate executives, politicians, and religious leaders.

There is already enough emotional labor required of us to confront our harm and endure the everyday experience of white supremacy. Having to increase that labor by navigating white tears just makes matters worse. I was talking to a white woman who shared that she was often a crier, and she believed that she could not control it. The deeper she got into her anti-racism work, the more she realized how problematic her tears were. She proactively researched and explored ways to withhold tears (apparently other white women had provided some advice and tools online, based on their own anti-racism work) and started implementing the practice. She ended her narrative by saying to me, "I realized that I *can* hold them in." The more that it became a practice, the more she realized that the matters she used to cry about did not merit tears at all. She recounted, "It's incredible how I would cry about things involving race that I would never cry about if it were the exact same scenario with a different topic. Why did I do that?"

I am glad that she noted this because it supports my declarations that I am not insensitive or hard-hearted for being opposed to white tears. White tears are a very particular category, and they are different from tears of empathy or compassion. I have shared some powerful moments with white people where I could feel their allyship and true human connectedness concerning matters of race. I have felt moments of incredible covering and comfort from white people who happened to get emotional as they held space with me and centered my Black experience. Compassion is different from white tears, and my lack of patience for white tears is not about "compassion fatigue."

My lack of patience for white tears is about holding people accountable to be mature, and to dialogue like adults.

It is about expecting people to face race. It is about expecting people to de-center themselves in conversations that are about others.

It is about people taking responsibility for their actions. It is about people understanding the damage that their reactions can cause.

It is about people learning tools to unload in private when necessary. It is about people understanding that their white privilege has conditioned them to cry about matters that they otherwise would not.

It is about getting people to understand that while the conversation about race usually stops once tears are involved, I am going to challenge them to push through.

Tears have power. So, when they are unleashed, I am now deliberate about maintaining my power or taking it back.

CHAPTER 13

REPETITION

I was partnering with an organization to teach anti-racism allyship, which involved working extensively with a couple of primary coordinators. One of the women was as sweet as pie—always willing to go above and beyond to see the work through with excellence, and intensely committed to the work. However, we had a difficult working relationship. Even though she was very supportive, white supremacy often crept in through her behavior. She often sought to correct or impose on my content, regularly overstepped boundaries with expectations of my time, and repeatedly cried upon being addressed. She was a perfect example of how intention does not always align with impact. Even though she intended to be helpful (which she often was), her behavior still created a lot of stress for me.

Working with her to resist crying in response to feedback was an ordeal, but she eventually got to a point where she could hold in those tears. However, even though the crying stopped, one of my biggest frustrations was repeatedly addressing her continual problematic behavior.

Since fragility is so common, many people think that addressing it is the ultimate progress. Because the occurrence of fragility often ends the confrontation process, many of us have been conditioned to believe that absolving that, alone, is success. Often, Black people's experience when confronting harm goes as follows:

1. White person does or says something problematic.
2. Black person confronts their behavior.
3. White person becomes emotionally fragile (cries, yells, shuts down, gets angry, or leaves).
4. Engagement ends.
5. Harmful behavior continues or the relationship ends.

I believe that a mature reaction should simply be a prerequisite, not a declared progression—particularly if the original behavior remains the same. I am often told that I should applaud the supposed milestone that is merely receiving criticism in a mature manner, and that I should address my own disappointment toward the persistence of the original offense. I interpret that to present as the following:

1. White person does or says something problematic.
2. Black person confronts the behavior.
3. White person receives the information maturely.
4. White person does or says the same thing a week later (and then the next week, and the next week, etc.).

It is perfectly reasonable for us to demand more. At the end of the day, if I am still enduring the same harm or disrespect that required confrontation in the first place, then I will not be satisfied with the repeated behavior. I find the process of repetition equally exhausting as fragility. Correct, someone should not be crying every time their wrongdoing is addressed, but that person should also cease the behavior so that confronting it no longer becomes necessary.

Repetition and unchanged behavior have become some of my most prevalent challenges in this work. I know that it is part of the process. It is difficult to break habits. I can imagine the intense process of disrupting ingrained behavior that has been accepted without question, or even the struggle of trying to act correctly but still getting it wrong. I hear that from white people often, as we grapple through tense periods of repeated problems. They say, "I keep trying and trying, but everything I do seems to be wrong."

I empathize with this, and while I cannot particularly relate in terms of whiteness, I know how it feels to think I can't do anything right when I continue making mistakes after putting significant effort into trying to improve. When I feel that way, I get to a crossroads where I have a choice to make: 1) I can stubbornly dig in my heels and claim that I am not in the wrong [when I am]; 2) I can retreat and stop trying altogether; or 3) I can work even harder and be even more vigilant in my attempted awareness and diligence about treading with intention. I try to choose the latter in my areas for growth, and that is my request of white people. I want them to be vigilant and diligent about anti-racism.

I wonder if that is my tension point. While the empath in me understands that breaking habits takes time, the Black woman in me is tired. I am tired of feeling like my responses to the simple things—the seemingly obvious things—must be on repeat.

1. Please stop interrupting me.
2. Please do not use that word to describe me.

3. Please do not touch my hair.
4. Please stop telling me to train with different content.
5. Please ask for my consent before handing out my personal information.
6. Please stop colonizing my work and claiming it as your own.
7. Please pay me for my services.
8. Please follow my instructions as your boss.
9. Please do not call me angry or aggressive for making decisions that you don't like, or for giving you instructions as your boss.
10. Please do not make me have to stand up for myself alone.
11. Please do not silence me.
12. Please do not take up all the space in settings that are meant to center BIPOC people.
13. Please just think before you act and speak.

I am still determining how to navigate the inner conflict of having patience while also holding people accountable. Again, circumstances often dictate my response. In some instances, the situation may warrant gritting my teeth and saying nothing. In other moments, I may gently remind the person to check their behavior. Sometimes, I am at my wit's end and must address the matter more sternly, and other times, the matter just warrants a stern response and has nothing to do with my patience. If I am putting this much energy into navigating repetition, then I hope that white people are willing to do the same to correct it. Privilege allows us to exist in bubbles where we do not have to acknowledge the harm around us, and that we are even causing. Privilege allows us to decide whether we want to learn, and whether we want to do anything about what we have learned. Privilege allows us to be partly in, mostly in, all in, or completely out on any given day. Thus, I think that dismantling racist behavior requires constantly checking white privilege.

Many white people get so fragile when they are confronted about their behavior because they are not accustomed to being checked in a world where they are systemically allowed to operate however they choose. Then, they often justify their reactions by blaming BIPOC people for their tone—particularly Black people, and especially Black women. They say that if Black women could give the feedback in a kinder way, then others could learn and grow. Somehow, responsibility and blame often turn back to the BIPOC people for honestly addressing the source of their mistreatment. The compounded toll of addressing this issue publicly through my trainings, and internally from some of my white staff members, became almost unbearable at times. Running an organization that taught on this exact issue, then having to deal with it in its strongest form internally, was demoralizing. At times, I found myself unable to make decisions or give instructions without accusations of aggression, attack, or stifling of their agency. And I felt confident that had I been a white boss behaving in the exact same manner, the backlash and defiance would not have been the same. In fact, if I had been a white man, all of the other aspects of my leadership that were rooted in care would have been celebrated as revolutionary from a white man, instead of expected as a default from a Black woman; and his moments of instruction and decision-making simply would have been deemed as leadership, as opposed to aggressive and power-hoarding coming from me.

I will often get into philosophical arguments with loved ones and activists about whether white people have the capacity to change. Many of my colleagues believe that they do not. They remind me that people are vessels of centuries of systems that have been forcefully implemented as conditioning. They remind me that most people will not commit to the hard work on themselves that is necessary when they do not have to. They are justified in feeling this way, and their reasoning explains why I often feel like I am talking to a brick wall when I repeatedly address injurious behavior. I resonated strongly with that skepticism when white staff members, who had incredible opportunities to learn and practice firsthand—and to get paid while doing it, furthermore—seemed to stay in the exact same place, and even regress, despite all of the guidance and grace that they were given. Or when the training participant cussed me out in the middle of the session, when the organizational partner refused to pay after services were provided, and when the former friend accused me of "reverse-racism" (#NotAThing) for addressing the repeated microaggression. In those moments, I certainly questioned whether change in those individuals could really take place, and it made me question the validity of my work altogether. Still, I think it can be done. Hence, my challenging white people is not intended to bash, but rather speaks to my confidence in their capabilities.

I believe that white people can dismantle their own complicity through tireless effort and infinite work. So, when I push or correct white people, it is not because I have lost all hope; it is because I know they can do better. They can do better if they are willing to learn and actively apply the information, not just receive it.

White liberals are not exempt from this work, as I have personally witnessed the repeat offenses thousands of times. For many, it comes back to the larger issue of breaking habits. Regardless of their political affiliation, if they have been existing in whiteness their whole lives, then it will be challenging to do things differently. Hence, it is why they get defensive when they are confronted, or have so much trouble applying the new feedback. It was feedback that they were not expecting, and a whole new type of reorientation is now required for them to proceed.

I find it most puzzling when the learning feels internally transformational but externally insufficient. I will often hear white people share how much they have learned throughout their journeys as they dive more deeply into anti-racism work. It is quite powerful and encouraging to hear them speak of the new vision that they have for the world and themselves. They will speak with so much hope and possibility, but then continue to execute the same harm as the week before, the month prior, and the year before that. That is where I get confused. Do not get me wrong; I am happy to hear that they are changing…I just need to see it. Please do not experience so much inner transformation, but then keep repeating the same damaging behavior. Transformation from the inside, out means thinking and feeling differently after gaining the knowledge, and it also means acting differently. Otherwise, they may as well not have learned the information at all because inner transformation without external change really means nothing to this Black body.

CHAPTER 14

ABANDONMENT

One of the most discouraging aspects of racial justice work has been coming to terms with the regularity of abandonment. People often leave my trainings due to surprise about its content and high focus on internal work. Many enter thinking they will be equipped to address the system and other "racists," but not their own harmful actions. When they are required to turn the mirror on themselves, their likelihood of departure is at its highest. People often leave during the "complicity" segment, or when I highlight concepts like fragility and tears. Occasionally, they will leave in refusal of participating in a two-minute role-play. The fact that people are so quick to leave a training on race can be indicative of how easily they will abandon the real work of dismantling white supremacy outside of the training walls and computer screens. Trust me, the actual work is much harder than sitting through a day of instruction and role-playing.

The most blatant form of abandonment is when people exit huffily in the most dramatic ways possible, or do not return after breaks. Sometimes I overhear them complaining at the lunch tables, or on the other side of thin walls, about how divisive I am. Other times, they will go ahead and say it to my face in the middle of the session. While it's disappointing, I am not surprised by their behavior. I understood that fragility would often lead to departure when I decided to do this work, knowing that it would put me in predominantly white spaces. I have allowed myself a certain emotional disconnect, given that these interactions are ultimately with strangers. However, the wounds cut more deeply when my own colleagues leave.

When I started my organization, I was the sole full-time staff member for the first four years. Hence, primary organizational leadership and involvement outside of myself included three buckets of volunteers: cofounders, board members, and advisors. In one year, members from each of those categories left the organization specifically after conflicts or discussions involving race. With each departure, I became less surprised. They had made it clear that they would not be sticking around. Some departures were slow builds after multiple discussions, while others were immediate results of specific events. Either way, I knew when they were mentally checked out. In addition to their vocal opposition, their discontent was all over their faces, in their furrowing eyebrows, tightening shoulders, and crossed arms. By a certain point, I learned to prepare myself for the perpetual possibility of desertion. One of the last departures solidified the lesson that I must be able to invite people into this work with hopes that they will stay committed, but I must simultaneously understand that at any point they could decide that they did not want to do it anymore. It was important for me to hold both, which isn't easy to do. Admittedly, there were a couple of times that called for members to be dismissed from the team because they did not meet the requirements to do and represent this work—but that is a different story for a different time and a different book. To be honest, a whole separate book is necessary for my reflections on leading an organization as a Black woman.

This work requires arduous labor—physical, psychological, and emotional. Accepting that I am pouring so much of my soul into this assignment, with the high possibility that it will be rejected or dismissed, involves a special form of endurance. I must demonstrate the urgency of this work, display vulnerability to create empathy and compassion through proximity, and also maintain an emotional distance that prevents me from breaking every time someone decides that they are over it. This, alone, adds to the burden of the mission.

Abandonment is real, and I have noticed that it comes in different forms.

FRAGILITY

If you are tired of me bringing up fragility, imagine how tired I am of regularly facing it. People often choose abandonment when they become fragile. They will claim that they are being attacked or that I am pushing away people who are already on our side, as if immunity from accountability is a condition for doing this work. Someone once said that they were angry with me, so they were done with racial justice work, altogether. I remember saying, "Can you be upset with me and still work toward anti-racism?" They said no and stomped off. Once, a person even said that they entered the training as an ally for racial justice, but because they did not like my training style, they were now going to be an opponent of racial justice. They actually said that they had decided to be racist because they didn't like my tone.

My goodness. I am still bewildered by how people who can show up with a declared commitment will leave at the slightest discomfort of mirror work. If people cannot handle having to look within, then how can we possibly count on them to handle the strenuousness of dismantling racism? It leads me to wonder if white people can really call themselves committed at all if they are willing to leave the work altogether upon being challenged. Quite frankly, I cannot trust a white person who claims to be committed to anti-racism work but can't be held accountable for their own role in the system. Fragility is exhausting, and it is one of the biggest prompts for abandonment.

QUOTA

I regularly come across baby boomers who share extended resumes that recount all the great anti-racism work that they've done. Often, there will be mention of having somehow been in the presence of Dr. King. Seriously, dozens of white people have stories of their parents taking them to speeches by Dr. King when they were in strollers—and have told me that they are great people by affiliation. One person even said that her mother was pregnant with her when she went to see his speech—and hence, she is a good ally because of her activism from the womb. I cannot make this stuff up.

Seeing Dr. King speak, being actively involved during the civil rights movement, or spending their careers as social workers, teachers, and lawyers for Black people are all narratives shared regularly with me by white people. I have heard it in the other direction, too, from millennials and Gen-Zers. They will name-drop the activists they follow on social media, post selfies at protests, and make long social media posts about all the ways that they address racism in their lives—especially by calling out the harmful actions of their parents, grandparents, and coworkers. Whether from older generations or younger generations, this "quota-bragging" is usually unintentional white savior behavior. As the heroes of their own narratives, they are expecting a pat on the back or "Thanks for being great." However, sometimes they will tell me that as context for why they are finished with the work: because they are tired and have done their part.

There is no quota for white allyship. As long as racism exists, white people will always have a responsibility to address it. It may not present the same for everyone, but I cannot accept a white person ever believing that they are finished. I cannot walk away from this experience. Every day, my Black siblings and I live under the cloud of white supremacy, and we face the repercussions that come with it. Thus, it is offensive to hear white people think that A) they deserve a medal for doing what is simply required of them; or B) that there's a finish line that they have reached.

In all areas of privilege, we must acknowledge that the work is hard, and it is important to do whatever is necessary to recharge and stay as healthy as possible. That is why rest, community, and joy are critical in allyship work. However, for as long as these issues exist, we can never feel that we are done. In my privilege, I must constantly remind myself that I can leave the work, but my marginalized siblings will continue to experience oppression. It reminds me that I can never do enough and that I must always stay committed. Allyship needs to be a lifestyle to which we constantly recommit. Hence, white people can never "arrive" in racial justice work. There will always be work to do on themselves and in this world. I should never hear a white person say that they have done their part with anti-racism, yet I am regularly exposed to that narrative.

FEAR

I have been at protests that were obviously first participations for some white people. Their eyes widened when we walked into open traffic to shut down intersections. I could tell that they thought the protests would take place in grassy areas, or that permits had been received beforehand. They were not expecting the scenarios to become so intense. I saw those same wide eyes when I shared testimonies during trainings about my experience in Charlottesville or the blatant risk barometer of this work. I see them tense up when they are doing personal reflection and group discussions. They start to realize that dismantling white supremacy is an intensive commitment that could impact their lifestyles, jobs, and relationships.

There is value when this clarity clicks—when people realize the gravity of this work and, thus, why Black people address it with so much desperation. I have seen this realization light a fire of fierce recommitment in some. It prompts deep introspection in others as they evaluate the full spectrum of risk, and the reality of how far they are willing to go. And for others, upon evaluating that spectrum, they decide that the work is not for them. White people have left the protests when the police showed up, and they have also left disheartening comments on training evaluations: "Thank you for helping me understand the work that is required. It makes me grateful for your courage, but I know myself and know that I cannot do this. I have a family."

The knowledge of the full required commitment was clearly too much for them. I once spoke to someone who had clearly abandoned the work for a year after his fragility reached its peak. When I confronted him about this, he acknowledged that his defensiveness had been part of the reasoning behind his departure. He also said that, if he was being honest, he thought he was committed when he started this work but realized that he could not commit to the required risks. Did he think that his honesty would make me feel better? It did not. Allyship cannot be done without risk. Risk is a requirement of the work. Sadly, when that is realized, many leave.

WORKLOAD

Many white people have turned away upon realizing just how much work will be required of them. Sometimes they will tell me that the time and energy investment was too high, and that they just do not want to disrupt their lives that much. They realize that being "all in" is not just semantics; that dismantling white supremacy takes regular intention, commitment, and effort; that they may have to significantly alter their lives beyond what they desire and what is comfortable; that they will have to question everything they have been taught about the world; that they have to prepare for the unknown by working toward a world that society has only envisioned, at best; that they may lose relationships and social standing; that they may have to be uncomfortable. Upon recognizing what true commitment fully entails, some people realize that they don't want to do it. When it goes from being trendy to actual lifelong work, people often opt out.

I attended a summit that offered an optional "pre-conference" day focused on race. It was about two-thirds white and one-third BIPOC attendees. To clarify, this was separate from the other pre-conference session that I mentioned in an earlier chapter (where the white woman cried after being confronted about her racist depiction of "dangerous Black men"). Somehow race often becomes the optional session as opposed to main programming, and that indicates plenty. At the end of the session, while discussing what was next, it was clear that the day had been incredibly transformative for many of the white participants. It was the first time they had processed the gravity and depth of white supremacy in their everyday lives. Finally, a white man said what many of the participants' faces had expressed: "What if I don't want to be all in? What if I don't want to risk everything? I have a family. I want to be fully present for them." He made it sound as if committing to dismantling white supremacy meant that he would have to sacrifice his relationship with his family.

I often hear this concern. I hear white people inaccurately associate commitment to this work as a sacrifice that extends beyond them and affects their loved ones. The work is all-encompassing, but it only makes us better. It sheds the covering of division, individualism, and ignorance, and it allows us to connect more deeply to our souls, each other, and the earth. Yes, there are always people who take on full activist lives that involve more risk than the average person, but that is not the expectation or request. The expectation is a commitment to actively seeking and building a better world. I know many white people who have committed extensively to this work, and still have thriving and vibrant family lives. Furthermore, I see this commitment passed down to their children, who think critically and love deeply. The false equivalency of morals and loss is a scarcity tool of white supremacy. That conversation ended with a Black man saying, "I have no choice but to be all in, and I have a family too." The mic had been dropped. That was all that needed to be said.

Everyone does not abandon the work for the same reason, and despite the various excuses, the impact is still the same. It hurts. I am still impacted by the departures from people that I have known, with whom I have worked, and with whom I considered myself to be in a form of relationship. They do not surprise me, but they still affect me. Each departure leaves me feeling like I poured my precious labor down the drain, and simultaneously kicking myself for investing the time despite my better judgment. Worse, for thinking that they would be different; for getting bamboozled once again by their use of the correct language, their emphatic expression of unwavering commitment, and their promise that I could count on them for the long haul.

I can shut down and shut out quite easily, and I could do that each time that someone abandoned anti-racism work. I could flip a switch that blocks it out and numbs the pain of their choosing personal comfort over societal justice, especially given the frequency at which departures occur. However, I made a deliberate choice about a year into this work that I would have to equip myself to endure harm to a capacity that would be uncomfortable and even detrimental, but that I would not disconnect. I told myself that I would digest the disappointment, and allow myself to acknowledge that it happened and it hurt. Furthermore, I told myself that it would be important to acknowledge because it was critical to share.

I cannot escape the repercussions that accompany my Blackness in this world. When it gets hard, I am forced to endure and persevere. Even the most "committed" white person always has the option to leave. That is why I have decided that I may not be able to control their abandonment, but I can at least make them aware of it by sharing my disappointment that they chose to leave instead of facing the discomfort of acknowledging hard truths. I can highlight that they departed instead of facing accountability, and they turned away instead of doing the mirror work. They usually do not like hearing that. It will often make them even more fragile, escalating their anger, and evoking overflowing tears. Sometimes they will stare at me blankly, determined to show their justification through this unwavering stubborn posture—and other times because they truly don't care. And sometimes, they hang their heads in shame, keenly aware of the truth that I am sharing, but decide to leave anyway.

I allow myself to fully feel that abandonment every time because I will always choose feeling over numbness. Numbness desensitizes us, and white supremacy thrives off desensitization and disconnection. Furthermore, as Black women, we have been trained to regularly bury pain for the sake of productivity, causing the generational trauma to pass through our worn and weathered bodies. Hence, my authentic feeling is my form of resistance. My ability to feel and still endure demonstrates exceptional resilience and measure. Abandonment is real and painful, and my acknowledgment of that does not make me any less agreeable (which is feedback that I often receive about speaking such truth). It makes me more honest with myself and others about the severe toll of their actions.

CHAPTER 15

ALLYSHIP

I could not express my full truth without acknowledging the critical role that white liberals play in my daily weathering, and in the upholding of white supremacy as a system…even despite their good intentions. This is not new information. In fact, I hear it regularly from activists, educators, and writers. There was a long period where, by day, I ran a nonprofit that builds allies for racial justice, and by night I was heavily involved in local activism. By day, I was teaching white people, and by night, I was on the front lines organizing with Black and Brown people.

Often, my activist friends would express that they could never do the educating part of the work. There is pain that comes with teaching white people about race—even the most well-meaning white people who seek to be part of the solution. It is telling that some activists, who risk safety regularly, view the training work as some of the most taxing. They often ask me, "Why are you wasting your time?" It is a fair question that comes from a wealth of historical and individual context. History has shown us that many white people will not fully commit to this work. History also shows us that if even a fraction of white people would deeply commit to this work in the necessary ways, then this world could be incredibly different. Personal experiences like the ones that I have outlined also give plenty of reasons for BIPOC people to doubt that white people will commit in the ways that we need them to. Hence, my activist siblings are valid with the previously mentioned question, and I admit that I often ask it of myself with each new batch of fragility, repeated injury, and abandonment.

Then I remind myself that I am working with hope toward a possibility. I know what this world could be if just a portion of white people showed up in the ways that we have asked and advised. While it is easy to get disheartened by the constant affronts and repetitious cycles, I remind myself that if enough white people actively dismantled those habits, then the transformation would be massive. I believe that this change is possible. Whether it is probable will be up to them.

To be clear, I believe in the power of my Black community, and have witnessed our collective impact. Our existence alone is already resistance, and to see what we have been able to create in terms of community, culture, and change across the diaspora is nothing short of incredible. However, I will not let white people off the hook. Yes, self-empowerment is critical, but I always say that it is not the job of marginalized people to dismantle their marginalization because they are neither the creators nor the primary enforcers of it. It is the responsibility of the privileged. Whiteness is a privilege. No matter how hard or effectively BIPOC people work, white people must be held accountable to work even harder to dismantle white supremacy.

Many of my activist friends do not like the term "ally." They prefer "accomplice" and "co-conspirator" because "ally" has become unreliable. Many white people will call themselves allies one minute and then abandon the next. Then they will come back when they feel like it—or not. They will be vocal and public when it is trendy, and then they will retreat into silence again when the headlines have changed. They will speak with all the right language in conversations and then attack, degrade, and exhaust their proximate BIPOC colleagues with their behavior. They will espouse a commitment to humility and growth, and then unleash full defensiveness when they are called out for the harm that they caused in interpersonal interactions.

Allyship has become something where people can be sort of in but mainly out, changing depending primarily on comfort. It is a fair assessment when I examine my experience with many white "allies" and note this lack of commitment. However, I consider the three terms to be synonymous. Allies should be accomplices and co-conspirators. Allies should be all in. Allyship should not be considered a stepping stone to becoming co-conspirators and accomplices. It should be an expected equivalency. One's political leanings do not determine this commitment. I have come across just as many liberals who have been challenging to my well-being as conservatives. I have also come across conservatives who have entered trainings with truly humble postures that are open to learning, and I have seen incredible transformation. I have also seen plenty of conservative people sharing a whole bunch of vitriol, and liberals whose actions demonstrate a continued commitment to the work. Political affiliation is not the determining factor.

I know that allyship from white people is possible because I have witnessed it. I have seen white people actively seek to learn by listening to BIPOC people in their lives, and absorbing racial justice resources. I have watched them say the uncomfortable points when necessary and engage in the difficult conversations with other white people, knowing the importance of using their privilege to take on that emotional labor and possibly influence others. I have watched white people commit tirelessly to the work in their communities, and within themselves. This didn't mean that they were without error; rather, one of the strongest indications of allyship was their willingness to acknowledge mistakes, repair the harm that they caused, and commit to a better posture as a result of their learning. In fact, the allyship that I have witnessed from many other white people throughout history, and in my own life, has inspired and informed ways to improve in my own areas of privilege.

The critique in this section is not meant to be an attack on white liberalism; rather, it is a charge to stay accountable to the constant work that is not eliminated or excused due to good intentions. I hope that it is motivation to stay the course and correct the errors along the way with the knowledge that nobody is perfect, and better is always possible. That endless growth and potential is energizing when I think about my own journey, and it also fuels my optimism that white allyship can grow in numbers as more people join (and stay engaged in) this racial justice movement.

I hope that the white liberals who are reading have decided to push through to this point of the book. I hope that they have felt uncomfortable because discomfort comes with allyship work. I hope that they have received this with my authentic intention: truth-telling for the sake of learning and progress. I hope they recognize that self-work is critical, and that they are humbly willing to turn the mirror on themselves. I hope they understand that inner transformation must lead to outward action. I hope they recognize that we do not need saviors, but rather their solidarity. I hope that they are willing to work. I hope that they have committed to being all in, and understand that they will need to recommit every day. If so, then this hope that I am working toward will be worth it.

And for BIPOC readers, I hope that this chapter provides additional affirmation and clarity that all of this is not in your heads. It is very much a reality faced by many of us, and I hope that the shared experience affirms and reminds BIPOC people that we are not alone.

PART 5

BLACK WOMANHOOD

PART FIVE: INTRODUCTION

I love my Black womanhood, and always have. Much of that self-love is thanks to my parents. Growing up, I had my mother as an example and cultivator of the many incredible features of Black womanhood: power, love, morality, support, and beauty. Her positive attitude that accompanied her resilience, her kindness that accompanied her outspokenness, and her curiosity that accompanied her self-assuredness inspired the notion that my sisters and could truly do anything. I had my father who grounded us in spirituality as a refuge and constant source to refill. He protected us and was simultaneously committed to instilling independence and empowerment in my sisters and I, so that we knew that our possibilities were limitless.

My Black womanhood has always been abundantly clear, even as my "Third Culture Kid" lifestyle moved me between West Africa and Latin America throughout my entire childhood. I still remember looking around in elementary school and noticing that nobody looked like me. When I moved to Ghana as a pre-teen, I had an immediate sense of "home." To date, that is the location where I have felt the most connected and joyful, and I am so grateful for the opportunity to have spent those formative years in the region from which my ancestors were stolen. While spending high school in Mexico City, the city was vibrant and a wonderful place to live, but I experienced some of the worst ongoing anti-Blackness to date within the school walls amidst a predominantly white Latine population. It was an early indication that white supremacy is global, and a reminder that Latin America isn't exempt from its history of European colonization.

I recall the blatant pangs of womanhood—overt and subtle sexism reminding me that society considered me doubly inferior. Throughout my upbringing, there were actions and narratives in most spaces that indicated expectations of my submission—that my body and mind were ultimately subjected to or disregarded due to my gender.

When I moved to the United States to attend college, I was immediately overwhelmed by the unique circumstances of the country. I always say that the United States is not exceptionally exempt from harboring injustice. Just like every society, the country has its flaws. However, the United States is exceptional in the unique way that white supremacy is intricately woven throughout the land—worsened by a society that largely thinks it is extraordinary, and thus will not address the deep embedment of systemic racism. I came to realize early in my freshman year that while I always knew I would have to work at least twice as hard as someone who holds identities as Black and a woman, the reality was that there was a third component of labor to consider: my Black womanhood. The merger is its own separate category that neither white women nor cisgender Black men can understand. I can imagine that other Indigenous women and women of color may have similar sentiments. Speaking solely to my identity, I can assure readers that there is nothing like being a Black woman. I know that applies to people in their own respective identities, but this identity is all that I know. I also want to acknowledge that my personal Black womanhood includes the privileges of being straight, cisgender, nondisabled, and Christian; hence, there is much intersection to which I cannot speak and must always consider as I continue the fight for our collective liberation. This chapter is my exhalation about the fundamental components of my identity: my Black womanhood.

CHAPTER 16

THE PATRIARCHY

I must spotlight patriarchy in a book about my experiences as a Black woman. While I am unapologetically centering race, I would assert that patriarchy more blatantly and boldly presents itself in my daily life because, in addition to being systemically embedded in society, men of all races can uphold the construct as vessels. That makes the pie of participation in patriarchy through privilege significantly larger (there are many more men in the population than white people). And quite frankly, while many white people may aim to veil or reject the notion that they can act and think in racist ways, plenty of men vocally assert a genuine belief that their dominance as a gender is best for the world order (and I recognize that women and other genders can believe similarly).

All that said, this chapter on patriarchy was necessary, and its nuanced delivery of misogynoir is my reason for addressing it as the first component of this Black womanhood section (with full acknowledgement that this could be another separate book).

One of my most significant observations about patriarchy is that it is deeply tied to ego. While ego can show up in all identities as an area for self-work, it seems to be one of patriarchy's core foundations. There is a pervasive notion that men know more. One time, after a truly outrageous argument with a man who was digging in his heels about something insignificant that was factually incorrect, he started yelling about the importance of respect. Essentially, my disagreement with him was disrespectful. That was the misogynoir component of the scenario: Not only did he have to be right, but the fact that I was vocally opposed as a Black woman escalated the matter and supposedly spoke to my irreverence.

It seems that many men can rarely be directly informed by us. While they can sometimes hear our perspectives and recognize our abilities, direct influence from us is often rejected and further criticized if it is in opposition to their assertions. Much of my life has involved internally negotiating between stroking men's egos and subtly nudging them toward the necessary outcome, versus choosing to stand firm in my confidence with full knowledge that it may be at the expense of the goal. And on the few occasions where I have had the positional power to decide on the direction that ended up being correct, they have rarely acknowledged that I was right—and hardly ever admitted that they were wrong. They glossed over that point altogether, or somehow rewrote the narrative to demonstrate that they had the solution or idea all along. And then somehow sandwiched between all of that was the fact that I was controlling and demeaning in the decision-making or instruction. These negotiations aren't solely reflections from the past, but processes that I regularly navigate.

That ego also shows up in the form of regular mansplaining. While that can seem synonymous with the prior point of claiming to be all-knowing, I think that mansplaining demonstrates the depths of perceived omnipotence. That's why it often presents itself as unsolicited advice, with no concern that their input may be unwanted, out of line, or completely off-base. Many men will explain plenty, but not want to be told much. If we show anything less than admiration for their knowledge, or appreciation for their advice, then we become the ones with the ego problem.

This mansplaining includes the space that's taken up. If a man speaks incessantly, it's supposedly gifted wisdom that we must endure until he is done. Then we often get man-terrupted (interrupted by men) shortly into our response, and the cycle resets with another monologue from him.

The interplay between even just these examples of ego's manifestations already creates a challenging situation for Black women. If we speak too much, then we are a problem. If we disagree, we are a problem. If we disagree and take the time to explain our reasoning, then we are in an even deeper hole. It's all so contradictory, and such a double-standard. Somehow, men can challenge or minimize literally everything that we say, commit to being contrary in response to anything that we assert—seemingly just for the sport of it sometimes, and other times as an unconscious default. Sometimes they'll be so thoroughly contrary that they'll even end up coming right back around to contradict their own original points. Yet, the pouting, defensiveness, and even wrath that come in response to us stating differing opinions are almost comical if they weren't often accompanied by consequences. The more that we hold our ground and stand firm in our convictions, the bigger nuisances we are, and the more disrespected that many of them feel. I won't even venture into responses to feedback or correction. Just keep multiplying the previously mentioned reactions. Basically, we're supposed to just be here to listen and serve with reverence.

The power of ego in patriarchy often gets shared between other men, but not outside of those bounds. Hence, it is often the case that if a man is willing to recognize that an idea didn't come from him, then it must have come from another man. As much as I will hear plenty of men claim to respect our knowledge, experience, and abilities, I have rarely experienced it in interpersonal dynamics. Often, they must either get there themselves or be convinced or shown by other men; and usually, they won't loop around to acknowledge that I said it first. Plenty of times when I have brought up good ideas, men have asked if other men within our circles or spheres of influence had shared them with me. Several times, I have outlined plans where men have mistakenly praised associated men (who weren't even present) for the work. After clarifying that I developed the strategies, they would act like nothing happened, or come up with backwards ways to explain their biased blunders. "I'm sorry" or "My mistake" would have sufficed.

There is no race associated with all of this behavior. The common denominator is gender. While ego isn't the sole pillar of patriarchy, it's a major component of it. Sometimes I try to decipher the roots of white supremacy and patriarchy by asking myself where there are similarities and distinctions. Similarities include a desire for dominance and a fear that any form of equity or equality will subtract from them—as is the case for many forms of oppression. However, my working theory (informed by many other brilliant scholars, activists, and people with lived experience) is that whiteness includes deep roots of entitlement to obtain desires by any means necessary—and then a constant fight to hold onto what was accumulated. By effect, that leads to power-hoarding. It is a self-centered disposition that expects to be the default and central focus (let me reiterate that I am speaking about the construct of whiteness, not people with white skin). Patriarchy has roots of ego and self-acclaimed authority, not just in positionality, but also in knowledge. It demands a submission and reverence that is messaged as respect, and the construct asserts that those power dynamics work in everyone's favor. That's why paternalism is so deeply tied to patriarchy.

I recognize that even those distinctions overlap when deciphering the causes and effects of racism and sexism. I will not argue with someone who says that they have seen the qualities interchange between the two identities because I have, too. Different forms of oppression certainly influence and interplay with each other. However, my own clarity about these motivational distinctions helps explain why men of all races—and sexual orientations—need to interrogate and address their patriarchy. It is no coincidence that just as we have seen the increase of white nationalist radicalization online, we have also witnessed the expansion of the manosphere alongside it.[26] This internet vortex of men demanding that they take back their rightful place of power and dominance isn't just disgusting—it is alarming. We have seen the real impact of how rhetoric can lead to violent and inequitable actions and outcomes; and as more people of all ages are recruited into this ideology, the more detrimental its effects will be. I have barely scratched the surface about the outputs of patriarchy by speaking mainly to regular interpersonal interactions. The harm certainly extends to employment barriers, safety threats, stripped rights, violence, and other negative outcomes. It is frightening, dangerous, and should be concerning to anyone who believes that everyone deserves to thrive.

Of course, I have been speaking in broad strokes to address high-level systems of which individuals are often vessels—as is the case for most of my assertions in this book. I understand that every white person doesn't ascribe to, think, or act on every aspect of white supremacy; just as every man doesn't do so regarding patriarchy. I understand that there are exceptions, and I have witnessed such exceptions in plenty of men. However, I want to note that most of the men from whom I have observed a better posture have also readily acknowledged patriarchy's pervasiveness, and their commitment to actively unlearning it. I can also say that many men who have displayed sexist behavior toward or around me have asserted that they deeply believe in gender equality and are always respectful toward women—and this argument is often made in response to when their problematic behavior has been noted. Notice any parallels in that language? [See the prior section on white liberalism.]

I imagine that there are some additional parallels between white people and men who lean more progressively politically. For example, just as many white people have said that they couldn't have thought or done anything racist because they voted for Barack Obama, there may by similar arguments from men about having voted for Kamala Harris in response to accusations of sexist behavior. Ironically, the 2024 elections convicted me to have a more exclusive chapter on patriarchy, after hearing the frustrating discourse in the lead-up, and seeing the clear and disturbing trends in gender voting demographics afterwards.

As readers may have noticed, I will unabashedly rant about patriarchy, and I am confident that women of many races can find aspects (if not all) of this discourse relatable. The reason why it's in the Black womanhood section of the book, in part, is to emphasize that we also experience these dynamics (not just white women). Additionally, this chapter is meant to highlight how Black womanhood means that our disposition to patriarchy results in compounded harm and targeted misogynoir because we are systemically placed at the bottom of the social hierarchy.

White men fall on the opposite end of that social hierarchy. White supremacist patriarchy is at the root of many of our destructive systems, and it continues to drive some of the most lethal and dangerous symptoms of said virus. It gives white men ultimate power—a power they seamlessly inhabit without even realizing it. Since they have never known anything different, I have seen how naturally many of them expect the right to do or say what they want without any repercussions.

For starters, I have seen how charm and charisma can advance white men so much further than it can for me. To be clear, I'm not saying that they don't work, as I have seen many white men work incredibly hard. I'm just saying that charm works as an advantage for white men in ways that it doesn't for Black women. We're expected to be likeable and to deliver. If we deliver but aren't likeable by society's standards, then we are a problem. If we are likeable but need support with some aspects of the work, then we are unqualified. Being likeable is an expectation at base-level, and being unlikeable is a detriment. It doesn't propel or advance us like it does for white men; nor do we have the option of unflattering personalities being forgiven because of our valuable skills. Charisma elevates white men, and it is allowed to demonstrate their confidence.

I used to marvel at white men's levels of confidence in spaces.

How they believed themselves to always be right; how they often self-perceived their mansplaining as a gift of bestowing their knowledge, instead of the paternalistic arrogance that it often was; how they could man-terrupt whenever they felt like it because they believed their interjections to be the most important matters; how they somehow took (or received) credit for any positive outcomes, even if they literally had nothing to do with them—and any mistakes or shortcomings were always other people's faults; how they could mess up thousands of times and never take accountability—nor face repercussions for their errors; how they seemed to always have the right to "fail forward" and face limited barriers, relative to other people; how they would completely shut down while receiving feedback, or would view disagreement as insubordination; how, if they wanted something, they expected to receive it; how getting their way was just the norm, and anything less than that brought on their criticism, stubbornness, or wrath.

I was fascinated by all of this at first, but the more that I realized how the systemic nature of white supremacy and patriarchy had been infused into many white men to create this behavior, that fascination evolved into frustration and disgust. The cries of stress and difficulty from numerous white men during the #MeToo movement and Black Lives Matter uprising glaringly showed their privilege, as many of them complained that they could not do anything anymore, or how "wokeism" made them fear that any action could ruin them. Many of them were not used to the collective outspokenness and pushback, nor to being held accountable for their actions—and that was the root of their distress (and often hostility).

I could discuss the interweaving of white supremacy and patriarchy for days. However, the topic of patriarchy is complex within my own community. I love my Black brothers, and I will always put my body and reputation on the line alongside them. I am well aware that the world sees and treats Black men incomparably to any other identity. Black men are demonized, vilified, and disregarded. Black men are fetishized, yet the same physicality for which they are desired and exploited is also weaponized as false justification for locking them up and killing them. Black men are profiled and cast with an animalistic label to condone their censorship, surveillance, and death. I know this, and in a world where all of society systemically hurts, hates, exploits, and fears Black men, I will love, support, and protect them tenfold.

I believe that this dynamic of utmost loyalty to Black men shows up for many Black women, and history has demonstrated our commitment. Black women took care of Black men after long days in the field during enslavement, and we have continued to provide nurture as refuge in the present day. Black women have fought and protested for Black men when they experienced mistreatment. Black women have put our bodies on the line alongside Black men for their justice, and have shown up on behalf of them to lead charges in support. Black women have even absorbed the backlash and attacks from defending Black men in many circumstances, to protect them from the retaliation that they would face if they had spoken up for themselves. I have witnessed these scenarios numerous times from other sisters, and I have participated plenty, myself.

There is a history of Black men being able to depend on us, to be covered by us, to be loved unconditionally by us, and to be defended and protected by us. This boundless support seems to have sometimes established a norm of expectation that isn't always returned. I will always be there for Black men, and I also long for reciprocation. I want them to acknowledge how our experiences can be different, and even compounded, due to our gender. I do not want them to interpret that difference as competition for struggle, but rather as motivation for further empathy and solidarity. I understand that Black men have unique experiences in the world that aren't always comparable, which prompts my compassion and support in response. I badly wish that more of them could apply that same perspective in return. When Black women experience racism, it is not helpful to claim that Black men have it harder, or to inappropriately redirect the narrative to be about one's own experience. That is not support; that is self-centering.

It is especially not supportive to minimize or completely disregard the injury altogether because of the inability to relate. That can be one of the most hurtful reactions of them all. Hundreds of times, I have been told that a microaggression or inequitable outcome was not a big deal, was an overreaction on my behalf, or had nothing to do with my identity or experiences as a Black woman. How I long for support in recognition of my unique navigation of the world as a Black woman.

I want to be defended from the racism that we face on all fronts, including its unique presentation from white women. I know that there is a violent history involving Black men facing danger and threat for addressing white women's problematic ways. However, it is a different matter when white women leverage their tears to strategically gain the protection of Black men as they spew racism toward Black women. That topic of social triangulation is a whole separate narrative, but I'll conclude by saying that it is extremely damaging to feel repeatedly overlooked and unprotected, in defense of white women being racist toward us.

Lastly, I want to be chosen over the patriarchy. Sexism is real, and it is a dynamic that comes with all races. Women of all races can speak to the sexism that they experience from men within their communities. Black men are not excused from that because of their experiences with racism. The disgusting language that I hear in the form of "bro-code" (with each other and other races, including white men) is unacceptable. Black men are not exempt from considering how their sexism shows up in the wage gap, expectations of gender roles, exploitation, harm, and degrading language. And quite frankly, it even seems that some of them are pursuing white men's full patriarchal dominance that racism denies them, as opposed to liberation for all Black people. That is tough to name, but it must be said to reckon with and ultimately rectify.

The privilege that patriarchy affords Black men means that they also have the power to be allies to us by combating sexism that shows up in other men. That applies to the white men who diminish and disregard us, to the Indigenous men and men of color whose own anti-Black bias treats us as unworthy of respect or voice, and to the Black men whose misogynoir is on one hundred by expecting us to take our place below them.

I would hope that if anyone should be there for us fully, it's Black men. I would hope that their lived experiences of harm due to their Blackness would help them recognize that we navigate this world in Blackness, too. I would hope that their understanding of oppression would unlock their compassion for how that must be compounded with the intersectionality of our womanhood. And I would hope that recognition of our constant care is returned so that we can all thrive.

I will always be in deep and vocal solidarity with Black brothers. They have my unwavering support until the end, and I know that reciprocation is possible because I have experienced it. I have had Black male family members and friends who believed strongly in my capabilities, and encouraged me to fully live into my power. I have watched Black men fiercely protect me amidst the barriers and backlash that I faced as I publicly battled misogynoir while leading authentically. And I have been vulnerable with Black men who listened compassionately, and held spaces of care for me to take refuge. It is possible because it has been my reality in certain moments and relationships, and that is why I am being so forthright.

Admittedly, I handled this section delicately, and even battled with whether to write it so as not to seem like an additional attack on my Black brothers. However, I concluded that if I was going to fully exhale about the dynamics of patriarchy that impact and influence my Black womanhood, then this important topic could not be neglected. I hope that this message is received with the vulnerability and honesty that was intended. I hope that it provided more clarity and depth about how intracommunity gender dynamics greatly affect Black women's lives. I hope that in speaking my truth, my loyalty and love for Black brothers are demonstrated clearly by expressing how intricately we are tied to each other. I hope that my words further clarify the complexities that Black women face, and validate and amplify what we have spoken about for decades.

There is much more depth to explore to fully unpack these dynamics, and I am well aware that Black men have valid criticisms of Black women in this context. We are certainly not exempt from the harm that we cause, nor from the ways that white supremacy and patriarchy can impact our psyches at the expense of our Black brothers. We should not be contributing to their dehumanizing narrative, nor holding them to unfair expectations that are rooted in our own biases or entitlement.

I also recognize that the gender spectrum extends beyond the binary, and that the Black community includes more than cisgender Black women and men. This section was not meant to exclude my trans, nonbinary, gender nonconforming, and queer siblings, but rather to speak particularly to my experience and observations with cisgender Black men. There is certainly a wider conversation to be had between the varying identities in the Black community, which I welcome and also seek guidance, education, and accountability for in my identity as a cisgender Black woman.

This reflection barely scratches the surface of the conversation that I hope can and will continue in community, care, and accountability with each other; and my genuine desire is for it to bring us into deeper unity and love as we continue pursuing our collective liberation.

As I bring this chapter to a close, I want to note that it is not an "anti-men" section of the book. It is an anti-patriarchy one. I don't want men to suffer at the expense of other genders. I want liberation.

Liberation means disrupting the social hierarchy that favors one group over others. That's what I want.

Liberation means that no gender experiences any form of oppression for their identity. That's what I want.

Liberation means us all doing our internal work to unlearn ways that we have perpetuated, upheld, and internalized oppressive systems. That's what I want.

Liberation means being able to acknowledge wrongdoing on individual, interpersonal, institutional, and systemic levels so that we can all work toward repair. That's what I want.

Liberation means that we all get to live in loving and supportive community with each other, in vulnerability and authenticity.

That's what I want.

Liberation means that we can all thrive in our differences. That's what I want.

Liberation means that we collectively do our best to create a society that works for everyone. That's what I want.

My same passion and principles apply to disrupting patriarchy as they have relative to white supremacy (and all other forms of oppression). I just want us all to be free, and everyone will benefit from dismantling patriarchy.

CHAPTER 17

THE EXPERIENCE

I took a Black Feminism class during my junior year of college, and my life was changed forever. This intimate class of less than ten Black women, led by an incredible Black woman professor, transformed my college journey and clarified my perspective. This course provided language for countless personal narratives that I had never quite been able to express, and built an intimate community through shared experiences. To this day, it remains the one class where I felt most able to show up as my full self in a nurturing, passionate, and powerful space with other sisters. We read literature from great Black writers as reminders that we stood on the shoulders of giants. We watched political news commentary from Black women, who named our unique perspectives in a climate where a Black man was competing against a white woman for the Democratic nomination of the presidential ticket. We listened to female hip-hop artists who addressed the patriarchy in our community. We discussed uprisings, we discussed our bodies, we discussed music, and we discussed O.J. Simpson. I have never looked forward to a class as much as I did that one, and every session breathed new life and power into me.

Over a decade later, recollections of my Black Feminism course still move me, and serve as an important centering point as I navigate life in this body and soul. Recognizing the gravity of my experience as a Black woman can be overwhelming. Acknowledging the uniqueness of this existence can feel incredibly lonely. Lastly, my daily adventures can be exhausting. I spend large portions of my days navigating the ways that I am treated, and my nights trying to recover from them. They are pervasive, layered, and perpetual. A few of those daily encounters include the following:

THE MICROAGGRESSIONS

Microaggressions are subtle or misguided comments and actions that people make toward individuals with marginalized identities, which are often rooted in bias. I named them first because people need to understand their severity. People are quick to minimize microaggressions and blame them on ignorance, but I believe that they demonstrate how people are vessels of systems. The world has institutionalized biases and stereotypes about people, which then embed themselves in unconscious psyches, which then slip out through seemingly tiny comments and gestures. Hence, a person calling me "aggressive" does not speak to their need for a certain communication style; it means that they view any form of assertion from someone in my identity as imposing or threatening their institutionalized hierarchal position or comfort. Calling me "articulate" may be meant as a compliment, but I am positive that the same person who called me "articulate" or "eloquent" in amazement did not go around saying that with such enthusiasm to every white person who spoke well. The underlying bias is the surprise that I am well-spoken and intelligent, and the privilege is the belief that saying such out loud should be met with my gratitude.

I could write a book entirely about microaggressions. Not just the countless inappropriate comments about my behavior or language, the backhanded compliments, the inappropriate boundary crossing of touching my hair, and the blatant targeting of following me around in the store to ensure that I will not steal. I could write a whole novel about the severity of actions like these. There is a reason Black women are dying at three times the rate of white women during childbirth in the United States. There is a reason our mental and emotional health are challenged every day. There is a reason studies can measure our stress levels at a significantly higher rate than white women's (literally, studies have found significantly higher levels of cortisol in Black women's hair, a hormone which is released from stress). There is a reason our physical bodies are aging earlier and faster (again, proven by studies)[27]—that we are losing life at an expedited pace due to merely existing. It is because existing as Black women is literally killing us. It is weathering away at us each time we are reminded that society views and treats us as inferior. It may not be a blatant hate crime, but imagine a rock on the oceanside. It is possible to remove that rock immediately with an explosive. However, with time, the steady crashes of waves against it slowly wear away at that rock, and it can eventually disappear. This is how microaggressions feel. They are chipping and wearing away at us every day, and the constant harm is weathering.[28]

Many BIPOC people do not like the term "microaggression"

because "micro" seems to imply minimal impact, and that reasoning is valid. I appreciated learning that the "micro" aspect of the word did not define the magnitude of the harm, but rather the harm that can be enacted through interpersonal means—because, to be clear, microaggressions are definitely severe. Separately, I have heard several white people claim that they do not like the term "microaggression" because they do not like their behavior being deemed as negative due to unconscious bias. This insinuates that somehow the behavior deserves a symbolic pass due to ignorance, which is problematic. I always tell white people that intention is irrelevant when it comes to impact. I am tired of hearing that because they did not mean to hurt me, they are somehow absolved of responsibility for doing so. Harm is harm, whether it is intentional or not. People need to understand that, and think before they speak and act. People may not be able to control the implicit bias that simply comes with being human, but knowing this information, hopefully they can contain it instead of taking away yet another piece of my sanity, patience, and health.

THE FALSE EQUIVALENCY

I must actively choose to call myself a feminist. This is not because I have a problem with the notion. I am proud to identify as someone who works toward women's and femmes' equality and respect. My problem is that feminism often isn't demonstrated in its ideal essence. Feminism efforts regularly center white women. When discussing feminism with white women, their priorities often only include issues that directly impact them. There seems to be a lot missing regarding the struggles and priorities that come with my womanhood, such as economic stability, safety that expands far beyond concern for domestic and sexual assault, health issues that directly correlate with systemic racism's toll, and an ability to navigate this world without the fear of being considered a threat.

Beyond the lack of consideration for all the issues that are included in my idea of feminism as a Black woman, it seems that intersectionality is also disregarded when considering how my gender inequity is compounded due to my race. My race makes my experience as a woman even more challenging. White women may face a wage gap, but Black, Latina, and Native women face an even larger one. White women may worry about being sexually assaulted, but Black and Native women are assaulted at much higher rates, and are often disregarded when in need of support for the trauma. In fact, the hyper-sexualization of Black women does not solely disregard when we are assaulted, but asserts that we wanted it. While white women's violations are often labeled as victimhood or survival, Black women's violations are often deemed warranted and desired. White women may consider reproductive health as a critical aspect of feminism, but reproductive health for me includes having access to thorough and considerate healthcare, and preventing Black women's significantly higher mortality rate during childbirth (along with infant mortality rates during and after childbirth more than doubling those of white women's babies).

Lastly, sometimes it seems that our feminism priorities differ altogether. I am aware that all movements come with various philosophies and tactics toward liberation. Even with racial liberation, there are different opinions about what it will entail and what will get us there. However, I have realized that a stark contrast when discussing feminism with white women often involves our relationship with men. As I shared in the previous chapter, I am in deep solidarity with

Black men. While I certainly have my frustrations with patriarchy, at the end of the day, I will actively fight for both my liberation as a woman and my liberation as a Black person. Furthermore, patriarchy shouldn't be weaponized to justify bigotry. That includes my Black brothers—cisgender, transgender, and fluid, to be clear. It is telling that I often get into arguments with white women that start with discussions about "feminism," but then cross a line when they become racist. They will make completely racist remarks about a "threatening" Black man, or a Black man that prompted them to cross the street due to their fear of his dangerous size. The conversation flips very quickly because I am not having that. Their supposed feminism will not justify their racism.

All this to say, I struggle with feminism, not only due to its lack of fully including me in reality (rather than ideology), but also because it seems to create some sort of false equivalency for white women. Being a woman is not the same as being Black. The hardships are not the same. The experiences are not the same, and it bothers me immensely when a white woman states that her challenges with sexism are equivalent to mine with racism. I am a woman and I am Black, and I can state firmly that the experiences are not the same.

I choose to keep using the term "feminist" because I believe in its essence. I also stand by my commitment to liberation for all people, which includes desiring to see all women and femmes thrive. My commitment to my Blackness does not subtract from my commitment to my womanhood, but it does mean understanding that I expect feminism to commit to the fullness of womanhood, and not just that of white privilege. There is a difference, and white women need to acknowledge that if we are going to truly exercise feminism.

THE NOT-SO-SOLIDARITY

I strongly believe in the importance of solidarity across BIPOC communities, and I recognize my responsibility to commit to it as a Black person (which I will address more in a few chapters). That makes the dearth of solidarity toward Black women incredibly hurtful and discouraging.

I have said before that pro-Blackness must be centered to achieve everyone's liberation, and that is with good reason. The construct of race has white people at the top, and Black people at the bottom. Hence, dismantling anti-Blackness travels upwards through other races' strategic placement on the social hierarchy, and sets us all free. That doesn't mean that we can't spotlight other communities and recognize the unique ways that white supremacy oppresses them. It also doesn't mean that we can't recognize our shared toll of racism, and unite collectively to pursue racial justice goals on small and large scales. There is power in that, and it is a fundamental principle in movement-building.

The fact of the matter is that there is work beyond this, part of which involves recognizing and addressing how anti-Blackness shows up in other racial and ethnic communities. People of color have spoken about the anti-Black rhetoric that's pervasive within their own families and circles, and people of various ethnicities have told me about how Black people are on the bottom rung within their cultures. And quite frankly, this isn't just hearsay, I've experienced it plenty, myself. I have been in BIPOC spaces where people have said heinous things to me or treated me as if I was beneath or subservient to them. When I tried to call them on it, I was told that such behavior wasn't possible because they were also BIPOC. Clearly, it was possible because they were doing it in real time.

I have also been in scenarios where Indigenous people and people of color made incredibly anti-Black jokes or used the N-word. When noting the harm and inappropriateness of the behavior, I was criticized for my sensitivity—and even accused of gatekeeping for denying them access to humor and levity. The manipulation—or genuine belief, at times—was an attempt to absolve them of wrongdoing, which ultimately perpetuated the anti-Black behavior even more.

Full racial justice work doesn't just involve dismantling anti-Blackness within communities of color, it requires active pro-Blackness. Just as I have been in BIPOC spaces where I was blatantly disrespected as a Black woman, I have been in spaces where BIPOC people took direct offense from centering Black people. I would hear claims of exclusion when naming specificities around Blackness, or I would deal with assertions that Black experiences were always shared by all BIPOC people and never unique to Black people. That won't get any of us free, and the more that all communities are able to understand the importance of pro-Blackness for full liberation, the healthier and more effective our work can be. Furthermore, why do people regularly expect Black women to show compassion and support for their unique experiences and cultures, but then reject, disregard, or take over whenever we try to center our own? The question was rhetorical, but don't worry, I will keep answering it as we move along.

Again, I know that just as I am charging other communities to dismantle their anti-Blackness, I have the same responsibility to address my own self and community around the ways that white supremacy can lead to bias and harm from our end as well. However, this chapter focuses on the specific factors that take a toll on Black women, and I would be remiss in not naming that misogynoir extends beyond white people. Sometimes people imply or assert that they get a pass on accountability for their own anti-Blackness because they aren't white. While whiteness impacts all communities and can show up in a very particular way toward Black people, it doesn't exempt Indigenous people and people of color from turning the mirror on themselves. And furthermore, it is important to recognize that while we have some shared experiences, anti-Black racism is very particular, and pro-Blackness is a must in the work.

By always trying to merge our experiences, we often get erased; and before you know it, once again Black women are expected to work toward everyone else's liberation with no reciprocation or even consideration. There is power in what we can do together as the collective global majority. Let's just not allow that broadness to neglect and/or hurt Black people in the process.

THE DISREGARD

I feel like I am constantly monitored and invisible, simultaneously. I still often tell myself that I must work three times harder: as a woman, as a Black person, and as the distinct combination of a Black woman. As much as I am trying to unlearn that unrealistic pressure, society regularly implies that the expectation is inescapable. I feel like I am regularly being watched: watched by others waiting for me to make a mistake, watched as some sort of fetish that intrigues people, and watched to see how I will handle the particular cards I am dealt. I feel like I cannot mess up, despite knowing that perfection is impossible. It seems that there is little room for error as a Black woman, or it could cost my job, my reputation, my safety, my freedom, or my life. What others may deem to be paranoia feels like required hyper-vigilance amidst the high stakes.

At the same time, I feel overwhelmingly invisible on a regular basis. How can people know how much we struggle and still let us? How can people see how we are treated and remain silent? I think about all the times in workplace settings that I was the sole person asked to go retrieve the beverages or clean up the mess. I have even been asked on several occasions by host organizations to clean up and lock up the spaces when I was their guest trainer. I think about all the times that I have blatantly been addressed disrespectfully, and people have remained silent or, worse, laughed. I think about the number of times that I have expressed distress and was blown off—told that I was overreacting, or not to get angry or aggressive. I think about how I have run myself into the ground with obvious disproportionate workloads compared to my coworkers, and how I received no support—or was still expected to take on other people's responsibilities in order to "help them out" or "give them a break," as I was literally drowning in tasks. I think about how all of these scenarios have remained consistent throughout my career, regardless of my role—as a service year volunteer, as a coordinator employee, as a manager, as a supervisor, and even as a CEO.

How can Black women matter so little, yet have the world depend on us in so many ways? How can we be attacked so regularly, yet no one even bats an eye? And why is it that when white women express distress, everyone comes running—even if at our expense? Does our womanhood not matter as much? Why do our Black brothers go to the ends of the earth to protect each other, but stay silent when they see us getting disrespected—or when the very same men that they protect are the ones who are disrespecting us? Does patriarchy matter more than our dignity? How can other people of color know the deep pain from being personally impacted by white supremacy, yet participate so freely in the anti-Blackness that hurts us? Does access to a form of hierarchy matter more than our liberation?

The disregard and invisibility are unique and hurtful. When we scream constantly about it, few listen. When we cry about it, few have compassion. When we are angry about it, then we are aggressive. It is a spiraling pit of just wanting to matter, yet knowing that we do not. Thus, the cycle continues.

THE STRENGTH

While much of Black womanhood involves being disregarded, the world has made it clear that we are needed. I know that my work ethic is one of my strongest skills, and that I can go, go, go without stopping. I have noted that this quality applies to many Black women. Is that why the world exploits us? Because we have such incredible strength and endurance? Or are we so strong because the world has exploited us, so we had to adapt? It is a chicken-or-egg question to which I do not need the answer. All I know is that we are mighty and powerful.

I used to carry the "strong Black woman" label with pride. I felt like I was living up to the legacy of Black womanhood, and that I was carrying my ancestors' torch. It was only in my adulthood that I began to critically examine this label through questions, thanks to much reflection and dialogue with other sisters.

We critiqued this label of strength. *Why are we so strong? What about society requires our strength?*

We examined this label of strength with challenges. *Why do we always have to be so strong? Why must we continue to endure hardships that require our strength?*

We validated the pressure to be strong: *If we are not strong, then what will happen to our families, friends, and communities? What will happen at our jobs, churches, and volunteer activities?*

We explored the possibility of choice with our strength: *What if we chose not to be strong for everyone else, even if just for a day? What if we chose to say no?*

And lastly, we expressed honest vulnerability: *What if we cannot be strong anymore? What if we just want to live? What would it be like for others to be strong for us, and for us to receive support?*

Those questions did not emerge from just one deep conversation, and are common in dialogue among other Black women. We frequently discuss how society devalues us, yet has unlimited expectations of us. We speak about how this tension shows up in every part of our lives. It shows up in our families as we are expected to discipline and uplift everyone, simultaneously motivating them to be their best, while also being their daily refuge and refueler as they recover from the harms of the world. It shows up in our faith-based spaces, as I look around at many Black religious intuitions with men at the pulpit and women running the entire operations behind the scenes—often as volunteers. It shows up in our volunteer settings, where we take on an overload of responsibilities and then also help others with theirs (often without gratitude). And it absolutely shows up at our jobs, where we perform excellently and take on extra work, all of which still implicitly seems to be expected for free.

You see this workplace dynamic when others take and receive credit for our contributions. You see this when our lists of responsibilities are disproportionately longer than our colleagues'. You see this when we are repeatedly asked to plan the parties and arrange the food, or expected to take on additional roles and projects. Sometimes they are instructed as assignments, and other times they are messaged as opportunities to be "team players" in support of other coworkers. You see this in the lack of promotions, even more glaringly when white people and men who have been there for a shorter time and have performed worse move up more quickly.

You see this when, despite all of the above—the extra labor, excellence, and expectations—we are not equitably paid. I have seen it in my experience while running my own organization. I started my nonprofit, in part, to disrupt these systemic barriers by having more agency as the founder and CEO. (Little did I know that the systems would present themselves most strongly in the position, as if constantly trying to strip me of power that I was not supposed to have in the social hierarchy.) Yet, I still had to fight for my own equitable salary with my board in the organization's earlier stages. Admittedly, that was when I built an early-stage board of majority white people and men, thinking that makeup would aid in gaining external support. Trust me, I have my regrets regarding that approach, and I know better now. I developed a training that receives requests from all over the country, and I still find myself fighting to get paid by prospective audiences on a regular basis. Frequently, they would share their budgets and expect us to meet them with the same quality of services, sometimes proposing payments as low as a tenth of our training fee. Sometimes, they would even hold off on paying us for months after the services had been provided. Even amidst the different scenarios regarding my internal salary challenges and my issues with getting paid for services by clients, I would hear similar commentary:

1. "We don't have the budget for that."
2. "If this work is so important, then you shouldn't be doing it for the money."

3. "This doesn't say anything about your value or worth, we just have to think about the health of the organization."

The systemic intersectionality of racism and sexism is embedded in these excuses. This nation's first experience with Black people was unpaid labor, and it lasted for centuries—longer than we have been free. Additionally, patriarchy's messaging drives the idea that women's needs come second—that we are always below men in terms of value and priority. Hence, the combination of my Black womanhood means that I am an afterthought, at best. The institutionalized bias toward my labor deems it valuable, but free. So, when I am told that there is not a budget to pay me equitably, I am hearing that I am not a priority for the budget of the very organization that I built, run, and sustain. When I am told that I should be willing to gift my labor and sacrifice my well-being for the sake of the common good, I am hearing a narrative that we have literally been told since emancipation—that everything matters more than we do, and that I should not only understand that notion, but also support it. And lastly, when I am told that such choices that disservice me have nothing to do with me, I strongly beg to differ. I am being told that I have no value at all, and that has everything to do with me.

Those examples are just drops in the bucket of the millions of hurdles that Black women face every day, and they are the reason why we must be strong. If we were not strong, then we would not make it. And honestly, if we were not strong, society would not make it either because we do so much of the caretaking, labor, and advising (often unnoticed or unrealized). I am tired of having to survive an experience that I should never have to endure. I sometimes envision who I would and could be if I kept my strength, but did not always have to resort to it; if I lived in a world that allowed me to thrive and wanted me to feel loved and be great. It is a dream that I hope will become a reality one day, but we're nowhere close right now. So until then, we endure.

MY BODY

My body is sacred to me. I understand her; I know her. I can feel when she is off. And thus, I can feel how she regularly navigates the trials of Black womanhood. From my head down to my toes, I can feel that my body is tired.

My body is tired of people touching her hair. My hair is a part of my body. My body is mine and requires permission to be touched. Furthermore, my body is mine and she is offended when one sees any part of her as an intriguing item to grab. I feel "otherized" when others impede my space for the sake of their amusement and wonder. My hair may seem unique, but it is not my job to provide entertainment or be a bucket list checkbox. Furthermore, my hair feels the impacts of this world's stress. There have been many periods where I experienced significant hair loss. I would search the internet for answers to the tingling sensation in my scalp, and the apparent disintegration of my strands. I went to dermatologists, experimented with countless remedies with my hairdresser, tried many products, and never got an answer. It is highly possible that the stress has manifested in my body, and my hair loss is one of the effects. So, no, people cannot touch my hair.

My body is tired from carrying the generational trauma passed down from my ancestors. I have a physical reaction every time I hear narratives about how enslaved women would breastfeed the children of plantation owners. I remember going with a friend to the incredible National Lynching Memorial in Montgomery, Alabama, founded by Bryan Stevenson's Equal Justice Initiative. We both got physically sick afterwards, and I am positive that it was the result of generational trauma being triggered as we stood on the sacred ground of spirits whose lives were brutally stolen. A shiver channels through me when I hold the fact that all shades of Blackness are beautiful, and that many shades—including my own—carry a history of offspring that were likely conceived from rape during slavery—offspring who were immediately considered merely as additional chattel because just one drop of Blackness deemed those bodies inferior and profitable.

My body is tired from numerous stomach ulcers that have formed since starting my nonprofit, where a significant part of my job involves training white people. It is stressful trying to explain that racism still exists to people who claim that we are in a post-racial society. It is stressful trying to convince people that I know better about my experience than they do, and that my people know better about what we need than the paternalism that often oozes from well-meaning allies. Once, I actually felt an ulcer beginning to form in the middle of a training while I was explaining to someone that the definition of reparations involved money—not just an apology, per their passionate argument. Yes, that really happened. They really argued that the dictionary definition of reparations was solely an apology and did not involve any money. I cannot—and neither could my stomach that day, literally.

My body is tired from knowing that so many men feel that they deserve a say over my reproductive rights. Not only is my body tired of fighting for her rights, but she is also fearful of reproducing. I fear the prospect of bringing a life into this world that will have to endure the trials of anti-Blackness, and the process of delivering a baby knowing that Black women die during pregnancy and birth at multiplied rates due to the neglect and distress that our bodies carry from enduring this world's oppression. I am scared to have a baby that is twice as likely to die at childbirth. I am scared to have a baby that I will have to give "the talk" about police well before they are old enough to drive. I do not want to be terrified about their safety for the rest of our lives.

My body is tired from the appropriation. Black women are often socially categorized as the least attractive or desirable race (just research the statistics of online dating preferences), yet everyone seems to want to imitate us.[29] We are undesirable, yet people are getting implants to enhance their backsides. We are undesirable, yet people are getting lip injections. We are undesirable, yet everyone is copying our bodies, our style, our music, our tones, and our vernacular. Anti-Blackness is real, yet people emulate us because we shape global culture. It confuses and infuriates me. We have carved out something so special to create community and beauty in a world that told us that we were worthless, and now everyone wants to take it. Yet, so many people don't want to acknowledge (and pay) us, nor do they want to put in effort to end our struggles. My body is tired from this tension of being systemically worthless, yet valuable beyond measure.

My body is tired from this constant marathon of enduring anti-Blackness, dodging the next potential damage that could come from an encounter with a police officer, disrespect in the workspace, profiling at the grocery store, lack of service at the restaurant, or a hate crime in the public setting. She is tired of constantly preparing herself for the possibility of this happening every day, even if it does not. I sometimes wonder what it would be like to wake up white and not be immediately consumed by the cumulative burden of anxiety, stress, pressure, anger, and fear that sets in seconds after I open my eyes. The disposition of not having to worry about racism is a large part of white privilege. I think about how it would be significantly easier to fall asleep if I didn't have to actively fight to shut off my mind every night from the trauma or disrespect that I just experienced, the worry about what is ahead, and the general anxiety about what is constant. My body is constantly navigating the cognitive dissonance of loving my Black womanhood while resenting the pain that accompanies it. It manifests as sleeplessness, and she—my body—just needs rest.

My body is exhausted from all of this. All of this creates weathering—weathering from daily offenses, from inherited generational trauma, and from the constant consumption of distress about what could happen to my loved ones, my people, and me. It has weathered away at my mind, my soul, and, by effect, my body. Barely in my thirties, I can feel how existing in Black womanhood has impacted my body. Particularly since the years of activism, allyship training, and organizational leadership, I can feel how this weathering has been accelerated. I often think about how, when Dr. Martin Luther King Jr. was murdered at age thirty-nine, his autopsy revealed he had the heart of a sixty-year-old.[30] I could not imagine the level of stress and anxiety that Dr. King endured, but when I am stressed or overwhelmed, I do often wonder how old my heart is now. She is much older than the span of time she has been on this earth, and I am actively seeking ways to reclaim those years and preserve the precious ones that are left.

THE TRAUMA

I have recently become more comfortable with labeling my experiences as trauma. Adopting this word has been a journey. Trauma implies severity, and I did not want to offend others who have experienced various forms of trauma by using the word lightly. I also held onto the "strong Black woman" title because I felt that naming trauma would somehow diminish my resilience. However, as I processed the events of my life, the current state of my heart and mind, and my shared experiences with other Black women, I was finally able to acknowledge that Black womanhood can be traumatic.

I am traumatized by the microaggressions I've experienced. I cannot stress enough how harmful and severe they are—how they chip away at me every day and erode my mental and physical health.

I am traumatized by feeling discounted in the feminist movement, the Black liberation movement, and the broader anti-racism movement. I am traumatized by having to prove and explain this repetitively, and I often feel like I am speaking to brick walls.

I am traumatized by the disregard that comes with my existence—from feeling invisible yet being expected to do everything. My fortitude has saved me, but it has also forced me to unreasonably endure.

I am traumatized by how my body has been, internally, an imploding hub holding the impacts of this world, and externally, a mere human-less vessel to be exploited for profit and entertainment.

I am traumatized by the past and the future, including fear about what backlash could come from the risk of speaking my truth in this book. I intentionally used a tone that was direct and honest. When publicly presenting around these topics, I often speak more mildly, knowing that fragility is alive and well. Many who have seen me present know that I incorporate humor and enthusiasm into my content, in order to keep people with me amidst difficult truths. There is little humor in this book, and that was intentional. I wonder how that will be received by strangers who are just becoming acquainted with me through these written words. Will they automatically categorize me as the "angry, aggressive Black woman"? I think about my acquaintances and friends who have never seen this side of me. Will they call this book out of character? Will they abandon me (and the work), too? I think about my loved ones, who may feel that I have overshared and opened the door to harmful critique and character assassination; or worse, that I have disappointed them for publicly revealing these thoughts. I worry about the attacks and death threats, and how many more will come my way when this book is released. It is difficult to get used to knowing that people want to kill you for pursuing anti-racism and liberation, and for speaking your truth in the process.

I am traumatized by the abandonment that comes with existing in my truth. So many people have left. I have lost several friends from conversations about race—on their terms, not mine. Actually, that is not entirely true. I have definitely walked away from some friendships when I gave myself permission to choose self-preservation over a relationship of continued disrespect and no growth. However, more often than not, I have made the mistake of assuming that our relationship would allow me to be more honest about race, but when I have, they have left—blaming it on friendship and saying that I never should have said or done something so hurtful to someone that I cared about. I am still baffled by how Black people can endure so much regular harm in relationships with white people, yet when we share our experiences, many white "friends" will leave and attack us in a heartbeat. After one supporter abandoned this work due to our strained relationship, he told a mutual colleague, "Whitney and I were great, and then Charlottesville happened."

How dare he? I wish he had said that to my face. Part of me thinks that he knew better than to say that directly to me because I would have clarified for him with swiftness how our relationship was strained solely by his consistent racism that I could no longer tolerate. That comment is proof that this is not in my head. It is proof of why I proceed with caution. Many people do not want to accept the truth of Black womanhood, especially when it comes directly from us. They will blame us for everything and find ways to attribute our conclusions to flaws in our logic and character, rather than take any responsibility. They will gaslight.

I am traumatized, and rightfully so. I love being a Black woman. I would not rather be anyone else. And yet, the experience of Black womanhood has traumatized me. It is a trauma that dictates how I show up, and requires me to evaluate every experience. It is a trauma that informs my actions and requires me to overthink every next step. I can rightfully name it as trauma, and I am becoming more comfortable with publicly using that language.

Indeed, Black womanhood is special. There truly is nothing like it. I hold the complexities of beauty, brilliance, righteous rage, pain, and strength all at once. I share this unique existence with Black sisters across the globe, and much of my joy and healing come from this profound interconnectedness.

CHAPTER 18

THRIVING

I remember immediately grabbing Morgan Jerkins's book, *This Will be My Undoing,* off the bookshelf based on the title alone. I knew that this sister would validate the toll that accompanies Black womanhood, and how much resilience it takes to survive it for a lifetime. However, I want to restate that I love being a Black woman, and am so grateful to have been born into this body. This body holds a spirit that contains power, intelligence, and intuition. This body holds a spirit that centers and chooses hope every day for the world that we could build. This body holds a spirit that will always have joy. Some people who have known me for years think that I have lost my joy. They think that, over time, I have been consistently phasing into a miserable person. I beg to differ. Yes, I am spongelike and have absorbed the world as I experienced it, and I have not denied myself from identifying and adapting to the truth that comes with the systemic wrongs that surround us. It is both challenging and transformative to name wrong, and to assume a lifestyle that actively works to promote justice. I have allowed myself to acknowledge such truths and to unleash the feelings that come with them, but that does not mean I am not joyful. Black joy is a staple of our culture and history: how we can still sing, dance, tear up, and turn up amidst all the mess that we endure. As I have navigated my life and learned from others, I have concluded that there are several necessities for me to not only survive my Black womanhood, but to thrive in it:

DAILY JOY

I must experience joy on a daily basis. Daily joy allows me to counter the consistent difficulties that accompany living in this body. As much as I can, I aim for my daily joy to exceed my daily harm, so that I am always operating at a surplus. Sometimes my joy comes naturally; other times it is a choice. Either way, I make an intention of actively centering it in my life.

Many of my daily joy practices are specific to my own character. My faith is at the center of my life, and my most prominent pillar of refuge is finding healing and love through time with God. I am also a musician at my core. I have sacrificed music at times for the movement, and I have felt just how much its void harms my spirit. I now actively incorporate music and singing into my daily practices as much as I can. I can recharge by rehearsing for my Praise and Worship team set, a car jam-out, or channeling the greats with just a comb and a mirror. I also love nature and hot weather, and one of my greatest pick-me-ups is a hike or walk along greenery and water. In fact, my team knows that I must fit in a stroll during my workday, not just for my well-being but for the organization's. I accomplish some of my best problem solving, innovation, and stress relief during that time. And sometimes, I "just walk off, not to pop off," as I like to sing as my own personalized limerick. Trust me, my daily walks benefit everyone in my orbit.

These are just a few individual self-care practices that I have identified as a personalized playbook for endurance and joy. Unfortunately, these can easily fall to the bottom of the list of priorities on any given day, and I always feel the impact when they do. It is easy to say that my time is better used by pouring as much as I can into my work and my responsibilities, but I know that I operate better when I carve out this time for joy. Furthermore, I know that I will not be able to operate in this work long-term if I do not integrate specific practices to regularly recharge. I am allowed to be happy, and I frequently remind myself of that. Joy is a good thing, and I have a right to actively pursue and prioritize it—even if simply with a comb for a microphone, and Whitney Houston's *Greatest Hits* album blaring in the background.

RANTING

I have jokingly been told that I am allowed one rant a day, which I usually exceed by 10 a.m. I am an expert ranter. I rant in my trainings, I rant to friends, and I most certainly rant to family members. I am constantly ranting. The topics vary, but injustice is usually at the center—personal and societal. While I see the justified eyerolls at times, I will continue ranting because I believe that external release is a healthy and critical tool for surviving Black womanhood.

Ranting is a form of processing. The brain is exposed to millions of things in one moment, and it can only process a few dozen of them at once. As I navigate the world through my lens of Black womanhood, my mind is trying to process multiple items at once. In a moment, I am thinking:

1. "Did that just happen?"
2. "What did they mean by that?"
3. "Do they realize what they just did?"
4. "Wow, this is wrong."
5. "How do I want to react to this?"
6. "How *should* I react to this?"

Those examples reference only a few thoughts at any given second, which often race through my mind as I try to outwardly maintain my composure. That cognitive dissonance of contradicting thoughts and actions grinding my conscious brain against itself contributes to my weathering. Furthermore, society is often disregarding, minimizing, or literally opposing what I am actively experiencing. It has been a journey to get to a place where I could validate my reality. Thus, my ranting is part of the procedure of putting the pieces together to understand what has happened. Ranting helps me process the world out loud through my own lens and voice, literally. It helps me gain clarity. I have reached some of my best rant clarity in solitude—just the mirror and me. Issa Rae's constant "mirror talks" on the show *Insecure* were incredibly validating. I rant to the mirror just about every night, putting voice to the ramblings in my head or imaginarily addressing the people who I refrained from reacting to earlier that day.

Ranting helps people get it. Admittedly, most of my rants are in front of the mirror, and I hope that insight can illicit some gratitude from loved ones. As much as they may be tired of my rant sessions, it could be much worse because my mirrors have heard more than anyone. However, I will say that sometimes my rants are intentional. I have chosen to release that side of me at times so that people can understand. I have trained myself to, generally, be solid and calm in front of people. Yes, I can be passionate and energetic, but very few people have experienced my true rage. That is why it would be ironic if it weren't so racist when people inaccurately call me aggressive or angry in conversations, because they have no idea. What they are labeling as "aggressive" is really just bluntness and directness—or even just an opposing opinion. They do not know my rage, and that is because I have chosen not to reveal it. I know how to hold in my anger, and I have conditioned myself with that skill. I was grateful for Brittney Cooper's book, *Eloquent Rage*, which acknowledged Black women's right to be angry, and how it is a powerful source that we have been able to hone and use effectively to push forward.

All to say, when I rant, it is often strategic. It is an active choice that I have made to share my perspective in its unabashed truth. When I give several rants in my trainings, I am not just "going off the rails." These are specific moments where I have deemed that a rant will reach people more productively. I make an intentional decision to give power, perspective, and voice to certain narratives and points so that people can absorb the conviction. Some rants are gifted glimpses into my feelings to drive points home. In those moments, I choose to forgo the privacy that I guard so intentionally in order to heighten my ability to reach people. Hence, although ranting is an emotional outlet for me, I also actively choose to "let her rip" for the sake of public perspective and understanding.

Ranting is a form of release. The driving motivation of this book was to be able to exhale, and ranting falls under that category. By nature I am private and guarded, which is probably one of the reasons I'm allergic to social media. I am not one to naturally seek support or to disclose my feelings. Arguably, this is an area for improvement because I recognize the value that can come from sharing vulnerably. Hence, ranting is a tiny personal step in that direction. I feel so much built up inside of me every day that I often want to explode. I can release a portion of that when I rant, sometimes even adding humor and laughter to what would otherwise have me in tears.

Sometimes I compare myself to a tea kettle. I am heating up incrementally, and when I start to boil, that whistle blows. Have you seen what happens to a tea kettle when the plug is on the spout while the stove is lit? Instead of a whistle blowing when the water reaches its boiling point, the whole kettle overflows. Imagine if Black women collectively had plugs on our symbolic spouts. What would happen to the world if we all boiled over? I don't think society could handle our fully released rage, and quite frankly, I don't know if the world would be able to operate at its current capacity without us being the backbone and providing stability.

Hence, I really think that Black women's rants work in everyone's favor. Instead of labeling them as negative, please consider them necessary releases that benefit everyone. That is why I rant, and that is why I will continue ranting—even if simply to my bathroom mirror.

BOUNDARIES

I used to pride myself on being a "yes-woman." I believed it was necessary in order to have a reputation of constant dependability and support. I would still consider myself someone with those qualities, but I am no longer a "yes-woman"—intentionally so.

Society expects—actually, *demands*—"yeses" from Black women. The world has been conditioned to expect our labor for free. Our strength and resilience have further conditioned people to believe that our capacity is unlimited. I have seen multiple forms of this twofold dynamic. From social settings to volunteer roles to work life, many of the requests specifically come my way instead of toward others in the room. They are veiled with compliments about my being Superwoman, and are riddled with entitlement to my time, labor, and proprietary content.

In the past, when people asked for my help, I always said yes. When people expected my time, availability, and labor, the default answer was also yes—even if it made me uncomfortable, or was at my own expense. Now I have a running joke with my mom about how many "nos" I have said for the week. I am not trying to be difficult. I'm prioritizing my well-being, operating in a manner that requires respect, and creating important boundaries in a line of work where people often expect my undivided attention.

Creating such intentional boundaries in my line of work allows me to implement them in my personal life as well. I am better at being honest about when I have reached my capacity, and accepting that I cannot do everything; and I have become more intentional about choosing where I put my time and energy. I have held back on being the first to volunteer to do tasks, and I no longer always begrudgingly take on the role when no one else steps up. I have allowed myself to also draw emotional lines where necessary, and to relieve myself from having to always be the caretaker in every setting. The horrible COVID-19 pandemic enhanced my physical boundary-setting even more intentionally, out of personal safety. Admittedly, on a scale of one to ten in terms of caution and fear during the pandemic, I was a strong sixteen, and I literally hid for a solid three years. While I may have taken the social distancing to exaggerated levels at times, the practice allowed for additional shedding of internal pressure to always be present and available amidst external expectations.

Communities of people can share the load and mutually pour into each other so that everyone is full. It is not solely the Black woman's responsibility to carry that. This "no" work is necessary, but it is still uncomfortable. I am still trying to decondition myself from a deep-rooted need to give as much as I can. Every day, I am still navigating the line of boundaries for myself while also trying to prioritize the values of collectivism, abundance, and outpouring. It is possible and necessary to do both, especially as a Black woman. The word "no" has become one of my best friends, along with "Sit down," "Don't play with me," "Just stop," and "I cannot with you."

COMMUNITY

It is easy for justice work to feel isolating, and for this identity to feel lonely on top of that. I sometimes inaccurately associate the loneliness of this work with my entire existence, when really, I have had amazing pockets of community throughout different seasons of life. Most substantially, I have three fantastic sisters. I am blessed to be the second of four girls, and to have three best friends for life whose love, support, and companionship are abundant and infinite. We have traveled the world together, grown and evolved together, and prioritized our individual and collective relationships from childhood to adulthood. My sisters are incredible supporters and role models, and I will never be lacking in community because I know that I will always have them. I have also had friends who cared deeply about me, and would move mountains to make sure that I was okay. Many of my closest friends have hardly intersected or interacted, and in some ways, I have been intentional about maintaining those boundaries between my different worlds.

I am grateful for the loyalty of my individual relationships in different areas of life, and I am also very grateful for community. Many times, people will ask about my self-care methods amidst such a demanding lifestyle. I usually flub up the answer because I am the first to admit that I am not great at it. However, I always state with the utmost clarity that I must have consistent community and space with other Black people—particularly Black women. It is healing to be around people like me. To be clear, I am an advocate of moving out of our spaces and building authentic long-term community that includes people who are different from us. That is essential to true social justice, and I believe it should be the work of people in their areas of privilege to leave their typical bubbles (in respectful manners), as opposed to requiring people in marginalized identities to always do so. The both/and of this position means that it is also critical for people in their marginalized identities to carve out safer spaces by building community with each other. In a world where we are always standing out as the "other," there is healing that comes from being in spaces where we naturally fit in. In a world where we are often silenced, there is healing that comes with feeling like our voices are heard. In a world where we spend so much time explaining and justifying our experiences and feelings, it is healing to hold space with people who validate, understand, and can provide the direct support that we each need. Community for BIPOC people is a necessity.

Whether one-on-one or in group settings, sharing space with others like me has been crucial. I have fallen victim to gaslighting. I have allowed others to get into my head and make me feel like I was the problem. Having other Black women say, “Girl, no,” and validate my feelings has been life-changing. Having other Black women say, “Girl, no,” and help me unpack something about my experience that I had not realized has been life-changing. Having other Black women say, “Girl, no,” and correct me when I have been in the wrong has been life-changing. Some of my most substantial growth has come from other sisters setting me straight, and I am grateful.

I have let my lack of self-assurance get the best of me. At times, I have allowed the world to convince me that I was small and unworthy. Having other Black women say, “Girl, yes,” and tell me that I was right has been transformative. Having other Black women say, “Girl, yes,” and affirm my experience has been transformative. Having other Black women say, “Girl, yes,” and relate to similar experiences has been transformative. They remind me that I am not alone.

Lack of clarity and confusion have left me feeling stifled and hopeless in the past. Having other Black women say, “Girl, I don’t know,” has been critical. It reminds me that we do not have the answers to everything, that there is still so much to figure out, and that I am in good company. We are doing it together, and we have each other’s backs.

I am so grateful for relationships that have truly been my biggest pillars of refuge and refueling. I have had several “squads,” and I think that every Black woman needs at least one. They are great reminders that we are part of a sisterhood movement that stands on the shoulders of giants—getting things done and taking care of each other.

SOLITUDE

Alongside the importance of community, I have come to appreciate the deep value of solitude. I handle this topic with sensitivity, recognizing how the prevalence of loneliness has become a literal epidemic post-pandemic, and I can personally attest to the painful impact of social isolation amidst my own caution during the period. However, "solitude" and "loneliness" are not the same, and I think that there is value in intentionally incorporating alone time as a practice. I have embraced the essentiality of solitude as a Black woman, and it has been vital to all aspects of my health.

The world is constantly draining Black women. It demands our time, our labor, our emotional energy, and our patience. Especially with the work that I do, so much of which is teaching, I feel like I am constantly bombarded with questions about what to do and how to be. Granted, I will take a well-meaning person who is seeking to improve over a self-righteous person who thinks they have all the answers any day. However, the constant requests, appeals, and demands can be draining.

I have heard hundreds of Black women speak to this, feeling like they constantly must be "on" and available to respond to everyone and everything. I think that is why we had a collective eruption of joy when Maxine Waters said that she was "reclaiming my time" in 2017. The simple quote captured many of our collective desires and needs. Black women need to have space to reclaim our time and energy in a world that is always extracting from us.

There is power in solitude. Solitude grants us silence from all the noise. Solitude allows us to rest when we are weary. Solitude allows us to focus when so much is taking our attention. Solitude allows us space and distance from people who are always overstepping their boundaries. Solitude allows us to emote authentically, away from a world that always expects us to exude strength. Solitude allows us to develop clarity away from a world that is spreading countless false narratives about who we are and who we should be. Solitude allows us to live into the fullness of just being. In those moments, we are free, and we are resting. Then, we can get back to work.

REST

I used to take pride in the fact that I rested so little. I wore the ability to operate on minimal sleep as a badge of honor, and I pushed myself to the brink against loved ones' concerns and warnings of burnout. I believed that I had to constantly be on the go, and that idleness meant that I was being inefficient or wasting time that could be used more productively. I have been going through an extensive process of trying to unlearn my unhealthy relationship with rest, and reading Tricia Hersey's book, *Rest Is Resistance,* helped illustrate the particular systemic implications behind society's expectations of Black women's labor.

I started deeply appreciating naps as quick refuels, rather than their sole purpose being to replace sleepless nights. I started aiming to get a full night's sleep, as opposed to using late hours as opportunities to catch up on work in peace and quiet. I even took my first work sabbatical and intentionally did not pack each day with tasks. Instead, I allowed myself to awaken when my body was ready, and I approached the days with leisure. I have not only felt how rest has allowed my body to recover, but also the clarity that it allows my mind, the creativity that it allows my imagination, and the hope that it allows my spirit. I have become better with more rest, and I have been able to contribute better to my loved ones and society.

I still wrestle with the balance between hard work and just enough—between the energizing nature of working toward progress and possibility, versus the need to prove my worthiness and value through labor. However, through my active process of unlearning systems, and through the deep care and advice of loved ones and mentors, I increasingly appreciate the vitality and liberation of rest every day. We literally need rest to function, yet many of us have been conditioned to believe that rest is antithetical to productivity. And while this is a challenge for much of society that ties value to work ethic, Black women carry a particular brunt as the deemed "mules" of society. Hence, rest is not only something that we need and deserve as humans, but prioritizing it as Black women is a radical and revolutionary act in itself.

These are just a few staples that I have recognized as necessities while navigating Black womanhood in an anti-Black and patriarchal society. Before, I used to say that I needed these to survive. However, as I continue clarifying my vision for a just and free world, I want more than survival for us. I want us to thrive. Black women deserve to thrive, and if we create a world where Black women thrive, then trust and believe that everybody else will be thriving, too.

CHAPTER 19

WHO ELSE?: INTERSECTIONALITY, ALLYSHIP, AND SOLIDARITY

I am reminded daily that I have so much to learn. In fact, the more I learn, the more I uncover that there is much more extensive education ahead. Our individual learning journeys are infinite. I will often say that truly "woke folks" understand that they only have "woker" to get when it comes to our privilege (and I still use that term because I refuse to allow society to, yet again, politicize and demonize something that Black people developed and popularized). We can never arrive when it comes to being effective allies because there will always be work to do in the world and on ourselves, and more to learn about injustices that we do not face. This is why I am quick to correct white people when they say they know everything there is to know about race—particularly white parents of biracial or adopted BIPOC children, or white people who have BIPOC partners.

While I believe that proximity provides opportunities for some of our deepest learning (to which I can attest in terms of my own education and growth through proximity), it does not exempt us from our systematized privilege. I have stories upon stories of parents and partners who believe that their proximity to BIPOC family members literally means that they know everything about race.

The most problematic white people are those who think they "get it" with race, and there are parallels with other forms of privilege. For example, think about the many men who have said that they could never think or do anything sexist because they have daughters or sisters. This is why I am quick to tell cisgender men to step back when they assert that they fully understand sexism, especially when their actions involve manterrupting and mansplaining to all of the women present. This is why I tell white women to see the larger picture when it comes to feminism—because while we share our gender, they will sometimes choose their power in whiteness over their solidarity in sisterhood with BIPOC women. It is why I tell Black cisgender men to broaden their perspectives on Black liberation, and to understand that such a concept involves all of us being free—not just Black, cisgender, straight men; and that aspiring to have the full power and authority that white men have is merely upholding patriarchy, not seeking collective liberation. This is why I remind other Indigenous people and people of color that while we share some experiences under the broad umbrella of racism, anti-Blackness is an oppression to which they cannot assume understanding nor exempt themselves from perpetuating.

I am hyper-aware of the barriers that prevent me from being included as a Black woman. That acute awareness thus requires that I stay vigilant about the limited lens and unintentional disregard that come with my own privilege. I maintain that race is at the center of institutionalized injustice, and I also believe that none of us are free until all of us are free. I believe that race should be centered for us to all live our best lives, and I also know that there are many injustices that I do not face. I am straight, I am cisgender, I am nondisabled, I have US citizenship, I am Christian, and I am financially comfortable. All of these are areas where I hold privilege, and where I have the responsibility to do work so that there is justice for people who are marginalized in ways that I am not. Allyship means recognizing my responsibility to do the work—externally and internally—on issues where I do not experience oppression. Just as I expect white people and men to be allies for me, I should be expected to be an ally in my own areas of privilege.

Allyship is often considered through binary lenses, and life is much more complicated. It is important to think about the effects of injustice on an issue basis, and also how that harm is compounded and distinguished when one exists in multiple oppressed identities—particularly race. Kimberlé Crenshaw famously coined this term as "intersectionality."[31] The term helps explain the complexity of my existence as a Black woman, and that charges me to consider the depths of intersectionality's application beyond my own experiences. How is Black womanhood experienced by gay Black women when we live in a heteronormative society, in which members of the Black community can also show blatant and severe homophobia? How is it experienced by disabled Black women when disabilities are often neglected in justice conversations altogether? How is Black womanhood experienced by trans Black women in a world where much of society invalidates their gender, and where their life expectancy is significantly decreased due to the physical violence, disparities, and neglect that they face? There are certainly levels of oppression in Black womanhood that I do not face.

Furthermore, there are levels of racial intersectionality that do not impact me at all. What is it like for a trans-BIPOC man, whose gender identity and masculinity are often ridiculed or dismissed? What is it like for a Muslim person of Middle Eastern descent? Islamophobia is fear, hatred, or prejudice against Islam or Muslims and is intricately tied to white supremacy because, while Islam is a diversely practiced religion, it is biasedly viewed as a Brown religion. What is life like for a Jewish BIPOC person? Antisemitism has been prevalent throughout history, and it continues to persist strongly today. Alongside that overarching discrimination, BIPOC Jewish people often experience exclusion within the community. As much as people do not want to bring religion and ethno-religion into the mix, we must recognize that religious and ethno-religious discrimination are forms of injustice, and that in the United States Christians hold the privilege. Christians can cause some of the most severe harm in the supposed (but inaccurate) "name of Jesus." It has been important for me to acknowledge that I can love Jesus and hold my faith sacredly, and recognize that the religion has been weaponized by many people to justify some abhorrent actions throughout history to the present day.

Just as I have spoken to the importance of Indigenous people and people of color being pro-Black, I must also be in solidarity with other races and ethnicities. The severity of Indigenous invisibility and erasure is undeniable, even when solely evaluating the implications behind the fact that Native people make up less than 3 percent of the US population despite being the original inhabitants of the land. We cannot disregard the brutal genocide that occurred against Indigenous people, and the lasting impact of this history. We must recognize the perpetual settler colonialism of theft, extraction, and cultural genocide that this nation continually drives. I could not possibly understand that experience—neither the intergenerational trauma that was passed down, nor the continued unique oppression that the Native community faces. Pro-Blackness and pro-Indigeneity must go hand in hand, and we must pursue our mutual liberation. That is why we cannot discuss the reparations movement for Black people without simultaneously prioritizing the Landback movement[32] for Native people.

I must constantly remind myself that white supremacy is global, thus so should be my commitment to dismantling it; while also understanding how that intersects with the lands that are now called the United States. As I unpack anti-Blackness and settler colonialism, I cannot neglect recognizing that Latin America had a similar history in the past, and experiences those effects in the present day. Society often confuses the Latine ethnicity as a race, which is both false and limiting. The presence of xenophobia and racism is complicated when we consider the varying and unique discrimination toward our Latine siblings, and how that can differ relative to their skin tones. Brown Latine people are often subjected to racism and xenophobia in the United States: discriminated against for their skin tones and villainized as strangers, regardless of their families' citizenship and longevity. As the United States continues to navigate the consistently high number of migrants at the southern border, I hope that compassion can be prioritized as we consider all of the reasons that people would feel so pressed to leave their homes, face the danger of travel, and completely start over. Seeking asylum and a better life should not be met with cages, family separation, or appalling narratives that dehumanize people who just want to protect and provide for themselves and their families. The recent increase of ICE raids and mass deportations since Trump's return to office further speaks to not only heartlessness, but sheer racism that drives many of these actions. Beyond the inhumanity demonstrated through ripping families apart and flying people to locations with no regard for their safety or livelihoods, it is racist to raid housing complexes and surveil neighborhoods with higher populations of Brown people; and to racially profile them in order to possibly uncover their lack of documentation. There is a base-level expectation of human treatment, regardless of documentation status, and we cannot deny the racist undertones and blatancy that play a substantial role in directly compromising that principle.

I must recognize that racism presents different motivations respective to the targeted communities, and that xenophobic racism is strong. I think of the anti-Asian sentiment and violence that have been present for centuries, and heightened as a direct result of the anti-Asian rhetoric that was spewed during the COVID-19 pandemic with false and racist claims of their supposed responsibility for the virus. Our Asian siblings often fight a narrative of being "foreign" and threatening toward power, as opposed to being just as deserving of a thriving and inclusive experience as any other human. I think of our Pacific Islander siblings and the complex implications of their Indigenous identities on the lands that were colonized, along with their classification with our Asian siblings under the broad category of "AAPI" (Asian American and Pacific Islander). By effect, they are politically positioned to often be neglected altogether in racial justice conversations, instead of centered for their unique histories and identities. I think of our Arab, Southwest Asian, and North

African siblings who are often targeted as dangerous, resulting from a narrative that was crafted by white supremacy to falsely instill a fear of threat to national security. A reckoning is necessary spanning thousands of miles, from the targeting of people of Middle Eastern descent in the United States, to the accountability that the United States must face for its role in the violence and oppression that was driven through war and imperialism in the region.

I think about my fellow Black siblings from other parts of the diaspora, ranging directly from the African continent, to the UK, to Latin America, and in the United States as immigrants and first-, second-, and third-generation Americans. I think about the context of their identities, and how they navigate the particular experiences of being Black in the United States. I think about the xenophobia that they face as "Black-and," and how Black Americans can perpetuate that xenophobic discrimination toward them in hurtful and rejecting ways. I also struggle with knowing that Black Americans are systemically perceived as inferior and negative by the entire world, and that sometimes Black immigrants in the United States are committed to distancing themselves from us as much as possible in order to achieve success. There is certainly continued work to do between Black people across the diaspora in terms of community-building, though I can also celebrate the power that we unleash when we come together as a people by embracing our commonalities and differences.

I must remember that race is a false construct that aims to categorize people for the sake of power, and that the real complexity of humanity cannot fit into boxes. Our biracial and multiracial siblings navigate this society in that complexity, relating to the experiences of particular races and cultures while also having completely different experiences altogether. I must remind myself to ensure their inclusion as we pursue liberation for all BIPOC people.

Dismantling white supremacy means understanding its many manifestations, and recognizing its shared and unique impact on various communities that are not white. My commitment to anti-racism must extend to all of my BIPOC siblings: Black, Native and Indigenous, Brown, Asian, Pacific Islander, Arab, Middle Eastern, biracial, multiracial, and more. I must hold myself accountable to education and solidarity, just as I hope that Indigenous people and people of color will do for me. The system knows that one of its highest points of vulnerability is solidarity. When marginalized people unite in solidarity, we hold much more power. This is why the scarcity mentality is systemic genius. The construct falsely convinces us that we must fend for ourselves, but liberation shows us that our collective power only yields more abundance. Solidarity is the way.

I am grateful to have witnessed solidarity in my own life. I have organized with multiracial coalitions, where sometimes we all fought the power together in collective struggle, sometimes we focused on matters specifically involving Black lives, and other times we centered issues and initiatives that impacted other communities of color. Our shared efforts exemplified how solidarity brings immense power, and that it is critical to collective liberation.

I maintain the position that when race is one of the factors included in someone's experience of multiple oppressed identities, it causes the most harm. Still, I also recognize that people can experience marginalization in more than one identity outside of race. An LGBTQ+ white woman experiences queerphobia and sexism, to which I cannot relate. A white woman with disabilities has experiences in a sexist and ableist world, to which I cannot relate. They are both still white and have white privilege, but they still face unique forms of compounded harm. Furthermore, mental health and neurodivergent conditions absolutely continue to be marginalized. Society is only barely starting to put more intention behind supporting people's varying neurological, psychological, and emotional needs, and it is not nearly enough. What is the compounded harm to someone with a marginalized identity who also experiences mental health challenges—or even develops mental illness as a result of their marginalization? All this to say, there is so much injustice that I do not experience. There is so much injustice that, in my privilege, I am unintentionally complicit in upholding through direct and indirect means. There is so much for me to learn, so much for me to improve, and so much for me to do. All of this is my charge and my responsibility.

I would be remiss not to note the particular resonance of my own words and responsibilities amidst the war on Gaza that is currently taking place as I complete this book's final edits. All of the complexities and layers of my allyship and solidarity responsibilities with race, geography, faith, and ethno-religion should be a constant conviction, and one example of that collective obligation has glared since the fall of 2023. The heinous acts of terror in Israel on October 7, which resulted in over a thousand deaths and hundreds taken hostage, were absolutely deplorable and can never be justified. The indefensible, reprehensible response of nonstop bombing, violence, and deliberate starvation in Gaza has killed an uncountable number of people. Given the demolition of the Gaza Strip and mass famine that will affect people for generations, kidnappings, forced migrations, and no ceasefire in sight, we will never be able to account for the likely hundreds of thousands of deaths during this time, let alone those decades from now. As I have stated, there is no room for neutrality when it comes between right and wrong, and what is happening in Gaza is wrong. This sequence has required me to be accountable to my values of self-education, speaking up for what is right, and keeping humanity at the heart of it all.

I have deep compassion for the victims and their loved ones in both Israel and Gaza, and for those still held hostage. None of them should be forgotten, but neither heinous action justifies the other. Nothing can justify genocide, and the systematic way in which that has been executed for almost two years is atrocious. The sequence of events has required me to hold the both/and of recognizing the deep generational trauma and the present-day harms that Jewish people face, while also fully supporting Palestinians' right to self-determination, safety, and freedom. It has required my outspokenness in critiquing the formation and actions of the Israeli government in contemporary history that have displaced and oppressed hundreds of thousands of Palestinians, while also firmly condemning anti-Semitism and anti-Jewish sentiments and violence taking place around the world—including in the United States. It is possible and necessary to do both, and assertions that critiquing one is oppressive toward the other by effect is not fair or true. In fact, it prevents us from pursuing holistic justice. In that vein, most recent brutality in Gaza has also required me to be aware of the full level of prejudice and attacks toward multiple communities, which includes the rise of Islamophobia and anti-Muslim hate crimes that should not be forgotten.

The ongoing and increased attacks on Muslim, Arab, and Jewish people are inexcusable. Geopolitical positions and discussions can and should take place in order to pursue justice and peace, without encouraging hatred and discrimination against any faith practice or ethno-religion. There is no place for Islamophobia, anti-Muslim hatred, anti-Arab hatred, anti-Semitism, or anti-Jewish hatred anywhere, and the assault on Gaza does not justify otherwise. However, this current season does stress that we must acknowledge and address how oppression is affecting specific communities, both now and historically.

We have been forced to recognize and acknowledge the violence and oppression that is taking place in Gaza, and the role that the United States' dollar has played in funding this war through finances and weaponry; and we must keep expressing our outrage and demanding change. This accountability should not solely entail a ceasefire in Gaza, but also a commitment to supporting its people's recovery, healing, and liberty from this egregious trauma. We cannot be silenced from speaking up against the inhumanity of it all, and I have been inspired by the organizing and allyship across generations, races, and (ethno)religions to ensure that this is not forgotten and that we stay accountable. I have witnessed how these conversations can certainly create conflict and divide at times, but also ignite learning, action, and change.

Every day, I wrestle with and explore how I can effectively provide support from so far away, but I need to try my best by learning, listening, and speaking up. As much as I rant about the silence of allies when I am on the other end of oppression, I must hold myself accountable to not become complicit in that behavior.

The ultimate goal is clear and simple: shared humanity and love in action are what we are working toward, through the means of justice. However, the work is anything but simple when applied to real life. It can be overwhelming to feel responsible for allyship work. Then I can easily become defensive, abandon the work altogether, or take an approach that is completely wrong based on my own inaccurate assertions of effectiveness. I also get it wrong plenty of the time, even when I have tried my best to practice the critical allyship principles of centering those impacted, doing the self work, and influencing others. Every day requires a recommitment to this work through intentional learning, deliberate unlearning of my systematized privileged ways, and concrete action. This is "forever work" that I must take one day at a time. As various human rights leaders have repeated throughout history, "None of us are free until all of us are free."

While communities absolutely have the power to drive and lead change, allies have a responsibility to show solidarity and actively do the work. Just as I maintain the position that I don't have the primary responsibility to dismantle anti-Black racism and sexism (it is a choice that I have made and a calling that I have answered, rather than what I owe to society), then I have the responsibility to pursue justice in my areas of privilege. This may not resonate well in a world that tells us that marginalized people must un-marginalize themselves, but it is my belief that such a narrative must be disrupted. If we can all constantly have a lens of "who else," then we can do our best to ensure that no one is left in the shadows.

PART 6

THE WORK

PART SIX: INTRODUCTION

One day, I told a white friend about "The Talk," a cultural conversation that many Black parents and guardians have had for generations with their young loved ones about engaging with law enforcement. "The Talk" outlines rules that many Black people follow when they are stopped by police, with the hope of remaining unharmed and alive. My friend's face held a shocked expression as I told her about the rules, and then recounted narratives of when I followed that protocol during my own encounters with law enforcement. She exuded immense compassion as she listened quietly, seeking to understand Black people's fears and without excusing the police officers' intentions.

"I had no idea," she said. She shared how she was raised to always view police as protectors, and never thought twice about calling them when she was in distress. She acknowledged that her experience was different from mine and, thus, never had reason to consider an alternative. She admitted that racism had looked a specific way to her. To her, racism looked like bad people intentionally doing bad things to BIPOC people. It did not look like good people imposing violence on BIPOC people, particularly in a role that claimed to serve and protect.

That conversation was powerful for many reasons. It was an example of how, in our privilege, we often do not know the marginalization that other people face. We only know our own experiences, which are favored and often accepted as the norm. During college I learned about many of our trans and nonbinary siblings' experiences with bathrooms, and it was completely new information to me. As I heard narratives about them deciphering whether it was ultimately safer or more comfortable to choose between the binary options of male and female stalls, I tried to put myself in their shoes. How would I have felt if I identified differently from how the world perceived me, or if my identity did not fit into one of the standard categories? What would it feel like to enter a space that aligned more with my gender identity, and to possibly face people who saw me differently? How would they treat me? How would I feel if I felt that I had to enter a space that did not align with my gender, for the sake of other people feeling comfortable? What would it be like to not quite know where I fit as I was still determining that for myself?

All of this is still an unfamiliar experience to me as a cisgender person, but I am grateful to have had the space to consider that my experience was different. My experience was privileged. There is still plenty that I don't know about what our trans and nonbinary siblings must face in this world, which is much more expansive than bathrooms. My brief education in college led me down a much more extensive learning path that I am still on today. I have been educated about the wide range of disrespect, discrimination, threat, and harm that trans and nonbinary people face throughout society. Still, as much as I may be informed, there are experiences that I will never have. At most, I will learn about them. At most, I might witness them. But I will never know what it is like to be marginalized in that regard.

It was important for me to recognize this as I continued my allyship journey in my cisgender identity. It was important for me to acknowledge that I don't know what I don't know, and that there are experiences that I will never have. It was important for me to understand that, given such context, it is my responsibility to listen and then support in the ways that are asked and expected of me—not to dominate with my opinions and assertions about the best solutions. It was important for me to accept that there are some aspects of the experience that I will never understand; and that I will still make mistakes and cause harm despite my best efforts.

I am still working every day to learn and unlearn when it comes to my straight and cisgender identity in a heteronormative world that oppresses and harms our LGBTQ+ siblings. I am still working every day to implement action based on this learning and unlearning; otherwise, it is useless in the larger scheme of things. Internal transformation is important, but quite worthless to our marginalized siblings if we don't leverage that growth to act and drive change. The same is required of my friend, who has a more heightened awareness about Black people and policing after she learned about "The Talk." The same is required of white people when it comes to race and all its intersections. Action is necessary: action in the form of dismantling ways that they may implicitly participate in the system; action in the ways that they support BIPOC people who are dealing with the impacts of racism; and action in the ways that they help influence other white people. The work is the charge.

CHAPTER 20

THE LENS

With each new level of understanding through my deepened work, my lens sharpens. I wonder if our hanging in the balance of what we can unsee or avoid, versus must see, is determined by our disposition to the issues. I see white supremacy because I am a Black person experiencing the effects of anti-Blackness. Even when I try to disconnect, I am reminded of it in some way, particularly as my lens sharpens to see that so much of the very fabric of society has white supremacy woven right into it. My chest constantly feels heavy from it. I have wondered whether it is possible for me to unsee white supremacy since I recognize that I am so deeply entrenched. Would it provide me with some much-needed relief, even if I could condition myself to disconnect circumstantially? At this point, would it even be an option to fully disconnect? Given what I know now, would I want to disconnect? Is ignorance really bliss, relative to knowledge? As I navigate a heavy spirit and a racing mind during endless nights where

I desperately seek rest, I ask myself these questions. I conclude that I would rather know, and that even if I preferred otherwise, my body would never forget because this brings on physical manifestations.

I cannot unsee and avoid the toll of white supremacy, but I must remember that I can unsee or avoid other forms of marginalization in my areas of privilege. I must maintain an active lens to identify other forms of oppression, even when I make mistakes or must face hard truths about myself.

We cannot envision a better world without identifying and acknowledging the problems. The lens is uncomfortable, but without it, all of this is futile. This lens means examining the past, current systems, and the infrastructure off of which they were built. There is a reason why mass incarceration was expertly referred to as *The New Jim Crow* by Michelle Alexander in her book title. She could not have put such precise language to it if she had not intensely examined how we got here.

This lens means investigating how we learned about the past, and the role that the storyteller played in framing our interpretation. We see some of the strongest opponents of removing Confederate monuments argue that it is an issue of identity—an identity that intertwines with a narrative driven by many Southern elders and history curricula that claim that the Civil War was driven by states' rights. That does not exempt other regions from this hard lens. Racism is not designated to the South, trust me. I had to debate the same issue in my high school history class in Mexico City. Lenses drive narratives that pervade and spread.

This lens means acknowledging progress while also considering what has morphed into the present as different symptoms of the times. Voter suppression may not look exactly like it did in the

1960s, but it is certainly still happening. While the Voting Rights Act of 1965 was meant to end race-based discrimination, it has been consistently chipped away at and weakened—particularly in the past decade—allowing for redistricting and increased restrictions.[33] The collection of testimonies from Black and Brown people about their registrations being cancelled and their voting polls closing is not conjecture, it is data.

This lens means truth-telling, even if it is uncomfortable. It also means doing so early in people's lives. Banning curricula and books in schools will not change the truth. However, its shielding is detrimental because it continues the cycle of erasure, ignorance, and damage. Everyone is negatively impacted by a lack of knowledge and diverse perspectives. BIPOC children deserve to see themselves in content, and to learn about the history of their communities. It gives them a clearer understanding of who they are, where they come from, and a sense of belonging by knowing that their stories matter. As much as parents and politicians may falsely argue that teaching about race in schools hurts white children by making them feel shame and fault, it does not erase the existence of white privilege, and it limits everyone—including white children. Race impacts everything and everyone, and the sooner that it can be acknowledged (age appropriately, of course), the better off everyone is. Diversity only makes us better, and fully addressing difficult matters together builds stronger relationships and communities. So, contrary to this argument of division, effective truth-telling provides our best opportunity to be whole and in right relationship with each other.

This lens means questioning and processing everything thoroughly. Not just who told the story and how that impacts the perspective, but also why circumstances are like this and whether there could be a better way. It means asking ourselves the hard questions about the current state of society and its institutions, identifying the virus and infection within those current constructs, and then reframing around the possibility of what could and should be.

The lens must be constant, not just evaluating everything around us but also within us. It must take place from the inside, out. The mirror work is a requirement. I have mentioned how some of the most fragile white people in my trainings are those who enter ready to teach everyone else, and then throw a literal tantrum when I charge that allyship also requires self-work. They can see all the harmful systems around them, yet they think that they are exempt. That arrogance will get us nowhere. In fact, it is detrimental. That same white person will agree that the criminal legal system is riddled with racism, but they will not have a process for checking their bias when they want to call the police on people who are living while Black. They will agree that Black maternal health disparities are urgent, and then not censor their microaggressions that further weather away at their Black women coworkers by increasing their stress and blood pressure during pregnancy. They will use "white-dominant culture" in their vocabulary, but will not examine their organizational and leadership postures to evaluate their own policies, practices, and power dynamics. They will praise the progress of the *Brown v. Board of Education* decision that desegregated schools, but they will be right back to advocating for school district lines that keep Black and Brown kids in one under-resourced public school system, and white kids in a better-resourced school for the sake of their children's supposed better educations.

We are not exempt from the system in our privilege, and our defensiveness and desires for comfort often shield us from the important lenses that we must have. A colleague of mine once said that she does not like the term "race-equity lens" because people can put it on and take it off as they please, like glasses. That point is valid, and it is also the very reason why I refer to it as such. In our allyship, we must recognize that we can stop doing this work at any point. I have witnessed that time and time again with white people in anti-racism work. Bearing in mind that privilege affords us the opportunity to symbolically "see" and do as much as we want, we must charge ourselves to actively recommit to using that lens every day, and to then pursue justice based on what that uncovering informed.

In many ways, part of allyship means making the choice to see the full picture of oppression, even if it's uncomfortable. Our privilege deeply ingrains us in this notion that we deserve comfort over everything else—even if at the expense of others in marginalized identities or positions. Hence, choosing the discomfort of truth-telling disrupts everything that we thought we knew in our bubbles of privilege. But you know what? Oppression is a whole lot worse. So, let's mature up, put on those symbolic glasses, and actively use that liberation-lens.

CHAPTER 21

DISMANTLING AND BUILDING

I have mentioned that people are always throwing their white-washed version of Dr. Martin Luther King Jr. at me when I speak truth to power and push up against the system. They tell me to remember to be Dr. King and not Malcolm X. This is a severely flawed argument, and it is incredibly disrespectful. For starters, their intentions behind leveraging Dr. King are misinformed. The real Martin Luther King Jr. was radical. He applied tactics that much of the country thought were dangerous and threatening during his time. Dr. King forced people to get uncomfortable. He organized public boycotts and blockades that disrupted business as usual and the status quo. He was revolutionary and unapologetic in his critique of society's ills. He spoke difficult truths, and quite bluntly at that. His bluntness is another reason why I get confused when white people tell me to be more like him, and not to be so "aggressive" with my words and tone. Dr. King was not one to water down his words or convictions. Yes, he said, "I have a dream," but he also wrote pieces like the "Letter from Birmingham Jail,"[34] where he talked about the white moderate being Black people's biggest stumbling block; where he talked about being tired of being told to wait. If people are going to throw Dr. King at me, then please throw the full Dr. King because my actions and philosophies are very much aligned.

Unquestionably, Malcolm X also played a monumental role in the rights that I have today. I honor and revere Malcolm X for his outspokenness and commitment to the Black community at any cost. Malcolm X was diligent in his pursuit of justice, and he provided a crucial lens and framework for taking back our power, investing in our people, and naming white supremacy. He forced others to note how systemic racism persisted beyond the laws and into the fabric of society and psyche. He unapologetically and unabashedly emphasized Black people's need to protect ourselves and each other, and the fact that we have every right to make that a priority. He did not mince words for white comfort, and his candor was spoken with clarity and confidence. He also acknowledged how Black women are disproportionately disrespected, unprotected, and neglected; and I am so glad he stated that publicly.[35]

I am grateful for Rosa Parks, a Black woman whose intentional seat on public transportation catapulted the power of divestment through the bus boycott that ensued; and who also contributed heavily to the revolution before and after that historic moment. She had been engaging in activism long before she took and kept that fateful seat on the Montgomery bus, and she continued using her voice and driving action into her later years. Her example reminds me that Black women's endurance and commitment are unmatched, and that we are often the spirit and strength of movements.

I am grateful for Ella Baker, whose collectivist approach to movement work was inclusive by promoting grassroots organizing, empowering people to advocate for themselves, and inviting young people's active participation. She held the duality of being a humble freedom fighter alongside other activists, and a vocal critic of the inequality and mistreatment that she witnessed in larger society and within movement spaces—even if it meant engaging in conflict and uncomfortable discourse (such as addressing the sexism and elitism that sometimes presented itself in organizing efforts). She inspires me to prioritize collective community work over individual advancement in my liberation pursuits.

I am grateful for Angela Davis. Just all of her. I am grateful for her unapologetic truth-telling and general stature. Her consistent afro and raised fist in the courtroom during her imprisonment, and subsequent trial in the early 1970s, showed that she would not be broken. She never made herself small. She stared down the system with all confidence in herself and her truth, and she won; and she continues to be an important voice in the movement. I strive to have her bravery and endurance—to have seen and done all that she has, and to still maintain her hope, passion, and commitment to the work.

I am grateful for Audre Lorde, whose poetic artistry combined with activism helped me more fully understand the impacts of my Black womanhood, and challenged me to go even deeper within that framing of intersectionality to pursue liberation for all Black women beyond solely gender and race. I am grateful for her words that "the master's tools will never dismantle the master's house,"[36] as they pushed me to explore means to liberation that were not confined under the umbrella of white supremacy.

I am grateful for John Lewis, whose loving and gentle spirit, fierce and disruptive activism, and political tenure demonstrated that we can have different personality traits and take many approaches to liberation work; that we are not confined to only one way of pursuing justice; that we need not fit into one box; and that life can take us down different paths in the work. I appreciate that his very existence demonstrated that love is not contrary to justice; rather, justice is love in action. I am grateful for his coining the term "good trouble," which disrupts such binary thinking through two simple words.

I am grateful for Bryan Stevenson, a humble man, and a motivating truth-teller and advocate. He has dedicated his entire life to supporting incarcerated people, particularly those on death row. While this has been his specific area of focus, he has leveraged his work to challenge the system through unabashed honesty and loving encouragement. His book, *Just Mercy*, is one of the most beautiful and transformative pieces that I have ever read, as he sheds light on systems while inviting us all into deeper compassion and improvement.

I am grateful for Harriet Tubman. When asked who I would like to have at an intimate dinner table, Jesus is at the top of my list, and she falls second. Harriet Tubman represents the epitome of Black womanhood: love, courage, resilience, care, innovation, selflessness, and so many other qualities. While she would have been fully warranted to pursue whatever path she desired for herself after escaping slavery, she dedicated her life to bringing other people to freedom through the Underground Railroad. Harriet Tubman, in short, demonstrates a commitment to the belief that none of us are free until all of us are free. Period. Harriet Tubman was heroic. Harriet was incredible.

I am grateful for the thousands of other named and unnamed faces in history who have contributed to my liberation—particularly

Black women and Black LGBTQ+ people. Jenn M. Jackson's book, *Black Women Taught Us*, pays beautiful homage to many of them, and further demonstrates my belief that not only have countless people contributed to positive change and social impact, but that such work involves numerous strategies and approaches. A variety of approaches will always be necessary for the most effective movements and change-making. The various tactics and philosophies of the civil rights movement exemplify that point, and those were built from the actions and thoughts of their own respective ancestors and influencers. As I think about my own philosophies and strategies, they derive from a plethora of approaches that were inspired by elders and ancestors spanning across centuries.

I am sure that all of my positions do not 100 percent align with those of other activists, advocates, academics, practitioners, and Black people in general. In fact, I am confident that many Black people reading this book may not agree with some parts, or even any of my perspectives. We are not a monolith, and that is a good thing. We will not agree about all tactics, but if our common drive is collective liberation, then the diversity of thought and action sharpens and strengthens our overall work. I continue to evolve, enhance, and pivot as I learn more, study more, interact more, and organize with different people. In just a few years, I can think of aspects of my philosophy that have stayed the same, redirected, deepened, and/or significantly altered—even over the span of writing this book. It would be arrogant to think that my mindset and approach cannot change. It would be limiting to dig in my heels so deeply that I could possibly miss a better way.

The binary lens of only one way is false, and boxes us into thinking that we are severely limited in our approach. It divides us and prevents our collective collaboration from reaching its full power. "Either/or" thinking is limiting and, arguably, an intentional tactic that minimizes the scope of potential for liberation. The grace in me will say that it is also often driven by ignorance. This is why I charge onlookers to reflect on where their feelings are coming from when they say that they agree with Black people's goal of change, but not the tactics. What tactics would they prefer to see? Is their reaction based on the discomfort of truth-telling? Is it coming from the rejection of mirror work? Could it even be solely based on seeing something done differently from that to which they are accustomed? I recognize that not every tactic is acceptable, but I would argue that many of them are effective and important in liberation work. Many of the strategies that would help achieve equity and liberation for everyone are often criticized and rejected due to being different, uncomfortable, and established as "wrong" by the status quo.

Just as the most effective movements were guided by varying approaches, the same will have to apply to our liberation. We will have to dismantle, replace, and build—and not on a straight path. It will be messy and disjointed. We will have to ask ourselves:

1. "What needs to go, what can stay, and what needs to change?"
2. "What will need to be replaced once it is gone, and what will need to be eliminated with no alternative?"
3. "What can we pull from the past as templates, and what do we need to create?"
4. And most importantly, we will need to ask ourselves, "What is the world that we envision, and how do we build it?"

That final question excites me. All the work gets us to that point. We are trying to build something extraordinary that allows humanity to live in abundance, joy, community, thriving, and love. I do not know what that looks like, and that is the beauty of this process. White supremacy confines us to the constructs of only what we know, with boundaries and limitations all around based on a scarcity mentality. Liberation allows us to stretch our minds and imaginations, and charges us with the accountability of working to achieve that vision. It also allows us to be empowered by the fact that we have examples of that from history that we can pull from. Everything does not need to be completely new; rather, we can build off of foundations and ideas that were already bestowed through our ancestors and elders. I have heard many older people express feeling dismissed and disregarded, which is heartbreaking and reminds me to actively address my own complicity in ageism. In addition to loving and seeing our elders, we must also remember that they have valuable insights through experience and wisdom that are critical ingredients to this collective liberation pot. Old minds are needed in this work, and young minds are needed in this work, along with minds of all ages in between. All are welcomed and valued in this movement.

The building does not start now; it has been happening. However, if it is a start for you, then jump on in. We do not begin once we have a perfect plan in place because that will not happen. Perfection is not humanly possible. Rather than waiting for the perfect plan, we should just get to work. We should evaluate what is around us, ask the tough questions, collaborate, co-conspire, start, and continue. Liberation looks like the active habit of honestly examining what has been, what is, what should be, how it could be, and trying to get there. The journey is the path, and I hope to operate in a manner that allows me to look back and see the progress made, while always pressing forward toward that dream world ahead.

Remember, dismantle, replace, envision, and build. Heal, celebrate, grow, share, and love. Let's get to work.

PART 7

HOPE

CHAPTER 22

HOPE AS A PRACTICE

It is understandable for one to see the state of the world and sometimes lose hope. This feels especially true for racial justice. Yes, there have been improvements, but when examining the mutated symptoms of this virus, this infection, I am reminded regularly that white supremacy is alive and extremely healthy. When witnessing how systemic racism continually rears its ugly head and grows two new ones whenever one is cut off, hope can feel fleeting. Therefore, I get frustrated when people tell me:

"Be patient; change takes time."

I often hear this when I share my dismay about the world's current state. Yes, this is "forever work," but there is urgency now. I am tired of others telling me that I should not feel that urgency, especially when my people's lives are at stake.

I try not to fault someone for times when they lack hope because I can relate to many moments of feeling hopeless when I reflect on the difficult period that we are in or the immense pain that society can cause. Hence, when that despair creeps in, I try to intentionally identify aspects of humanity that demonstrate that people can be genuinely good at heart. We have witnessed countless moments throughout history and in the present day of people operating from true dispositions of love and community. From the large movements to the individual acts of kindness and generosity, humanity really does have the potential to center good over bad. My question becomes whether enough people will do this when risk is involved.

I spend my days training people—majority white—to be racial justice allies. In my activism, I spent many nights risking safety with Black and Brown siblings who were prepared to make the ultimate sacrifice for the sake of justice. I will reiterate that we all wanted to live in those moments. To date, I still haven't sought an inkling of martyrdom. We just understood that this work came with risks. Often, I would go to protests directly after leading my trainings. It was a mind trip to make the drastic jump from convincing tearful white people that they would be okay after having difficult conversations with their family members about race, to developing emergency plans with fellow activists in case circumstances went awry.

This contrast often made me question: Do the outcomes outweigh the outputs? Will enough people really make the intensive commitment that is required to dismantle white supremacy?

The verdict is still out on that one, and, admittedly, my opinion frequently wavers. Thus, I have determined that my work is toward a hopeful possibility. I have hope that if enough people fully commit to this work, then we will experience transformative change—and that is what I'm pursuing. The potential is there, and humanity has the charge to meet it. It is easy for me to lean toward a more disappointing verdict every time the person who enters the training with so much fire about anti-racism is the first to leave within the hour, with their fragility at level ten. Then possibility is restored upon recalling incredible moments when allies risked everything for racial justice, and one of my strongest personal examples was in Charlottesville on that horrible historic day.

Discussing Charlottesville can be traumatic, and there are still some parts that I don't even mention. Charlottesville conversations move within my body in indescribable ways. I don't want to suggest that my entire philosophy is based solely on that experience. Thirty-plus years in this body and in the world have informed my current disposition, and I hope that an additional sixty-plus years in the future will deepen and sharpen my perspective.

Charlottesville was incredibly influential, and it is now part of my personal narrative. I also see how sharing my experience in Charlottesville impacts people, and I handle that with as much responsibility and care as I can. It can be a powerful teaching moment for others by proxy, and it was a significant one for me through direct involvement. There were many lessons from Charlottesville, and a significant one was hopeful: people will show up and risk for the sake of morality.

There were numerous non-Black allies in Charlottesville as counter-protesters who were willing to put their bodies on the line in solidarity. Two white people drove me to Charlottesville and didn't leave my side the entire time. Strangers did that to protect me—to prioritize my safety and lead over theirs. I must remind myself of that during times when I doubt whether enough allies are truly willing to risk something for the sake of our liberation. In Charlottesville, I was able to personally witness that at least some will, and I am convinced that the day would have gone significantly worse had there not been so many allies standing in solidarity out there with us. Allyship means assuming the risk of the marginalized while understanding that such privilege being present subtracts risk in many scenarios.

Still, people were hurt. People died. Heather Heyer died as a white ally when she was struck by a car in an act of terror. I extend heartfelt condolences to her family. I am so grateful for her courage, and I am so sorry that she was lost. It never should have happened. My heart goes out to the dozens of people, BIPOC and white, who were physically harmed in that attack and on that day. I hope that they can experience as much healing as possible in all aspects, including physically. I am well aware that my scars were psychological and emotional, not physical.

Allies showed up in one of the highest forms of solidarity. They put their lives on the line. This direct witness is an example that keeps me working from a hopeful disposition. Admittedly, my optimism can be fleeting in the day-to-day. Thus, for the sake of my spirit and longevity in this work, I have adopted hope as a daily practice. People often unrealistically expect Black people to constantly show grace and hope. Even grace has been weaponized when we are attacked and judged for prioritizing our rightful rage and hurt over forgiveness. I have seen society criticize Black people who doubt the likelihood of change. Frankly, there are centuries of context for Black people to be skeptical.

I have also seen people criticize Black people who show doubt in isolated moments, amidst track records of faith and magnanimity. Some days, I have renewed energy for the potential of what this world could become. Other days, I seriously question the effectiveness of my work. I used to be self-critical when doubt crept in. I felt that something was wrong with me, or that I was changing for the worse due to my honesty about its difficulty and the uphill mountain that we were climbing. People's critiques of my supposed evolving character would deepen my guilt. Any time that I expressed rage or doubt, I was told that I was not the "happy Whitney" that they once knew and that I had lost my "spark." People would often tell me that one of the biggest shifts in my personality was a loss of hope, and I would take it to heart. The guilt would compound into resentment toward who the world and this work had turned me into—who I had lost.

It took a while to fully unpack the inaccuracy of people's assumptions about me. People were mistakenly asserting that hopefulness is a personality type, and that my personality—the essence of my core—was altered because I expressed despair or distrust at times. However, hope is not a personality. Hope is a disposition based on our desires for the world, and their potential for being actualized. That disposition can be circumstantial.

Hope is work. I can acknowledge that systemic racism brings valid doubts, and that we can also have a disposition that believes in the power of transformation. This posture of hope doesn't always come naturally. Quite frankly, it cannot come naturally if we merely exist in the systems that society has created. Rather, the very notion of hope requires action on our part. Gone is my mentality that we are all hopeful until society breaks us. Instead, I now understand that pursuing a better civilization requires an active posture. Hope is a goal that we must actively work toward, bit by bit. I can accept that optimal change will not come in my lifetime, but much of it can. I can acknowledge that I don't know what a decade, or even a year from now, will look like; but I can take it one day at a time. I can take on a stance that actively tries to make the most of my current day so that tomorrow can be better.

It has been empowering to embrace and apply a concept of hope that feels manageable. It allows me to acknowledge and embrace feelings of sorrow and defeat in moments, without succumbing to guilt about my attitude. It allows me to envision a more tangible possibility against the seemingly abstract helpless state of the world, and to also apply this hopeful disposition toward people. It could be easy to presume that some people are just so far gone, based on their beliefs and behaviors. It could be easy to say, "They will never come along." I have often heard training participants express similar sentiments about loved ones who seem stuck in their ways, despite many attempts to engage them. My response is that I think many people are open to new perspectives. The pervasiveness of white supremacy can be so foreign to people that it shocks their systems, and can cause many to abandon or dig their heels. But I have also seen many people transform with a willing posture to learn more. Additionally, while I can doubt someone's ability to come along at times, I recognize that I have also often been the one who needed that self improvement. I cringe at some of my past thoughts and actions from positions of privilege, and I deeply appreciate people's grace, patience, and rightful reactions of hurt and anger that have profoundly influenced my thoughts and behavior.

I am infinitely thankful for how much I have learned and grown throughout my personal justice journey. I am boundlessly grateful for how that growth has impacted my daily actions and, hopefully, decreased the level of damage that I inflict. I often say that if we could all just prevent the potential daily harms, then we could collectively enact a significant societal shift. That is not the full solution by any stretch of the imagination, but it would be progress. We must proactively commit to the long-term and difficult work of dismantling harmful systems and building completely new ones. However, tomorrow can be so much better when each of us commits to being the best that we can today. If we all believe that we have the potential to do that, then we can collectively build better tomorrows, one day at a time.

CHAPTER 23

COMPASSION TO CONVICTION

As I have stated, I wrote and rewrote this book for several years, and kept editing until it finally got published. This section of hope was written a mere two weeks after George Floyd's murder at the hands of police. Society watched as a white officer sucked the life out of this Black man over the course of over nine minutes while kneeling on his neck. His murder compounded the mourning and rage from news just weeks prior of Breonna Taylor being riddled with bullets by police who intruded her home with a no-knock warrant, and the modern-day lynching of Ahmaud Arbery by three white men who had chased him down for jogging while Black. The trauma deepens with every name and video that's added to the list. The wounds were still fresh, and even with this book published or read years later, this next section is a part of my heart from that time.

June, 2020:

There are no words that can fully express the impact of George Floyd's murder. I only shared snippets of my feelings as I answered calls and expectations to respond publicly as an activist and organizational leader, and continued training others with tools to effectively show up as allies. Those isolated two weeks were too much, and as I actively process that period, I recognize that I sacrificed my own well-being for the sake of public demand and self-perceived responsibility. Still, in all of the trainings, op-eds, interviews, and discussions, there was never a moment where I completely let anyone in on the magnitude of my agony. However, I did make a deliberate choice to share parts of my reaction to my organization's listserv. Many people were expecting an "allyship toolkit." Instead, I spoke to them more directly. Here is what I said:

I am writing this message as a Black woman. I came off a solemn but restful Memorial Day weekend to news of the blatant and brutal reminders of anti-Black racism—a reality that has, in many ways, shaped my entire life in this Black body. I watched, with aggravation, the video of a white woman weaponizing her ability to call the police on an African American man in Central Park. Her tone made clear that she knew such actions carried high threat.

And then, I heard about George Floyd.

As I gathered information about his brutal killing at the hands of police, I simultaneously tried to avoid the traumatizing video that captured it. However, my attempts proved futile amidst the inundation of social media posts and news coverage. His cries, "I can't breathe," triggered traumatic memories of Eric Garner desperately uttering the same words before his death just six years prior.

I have been wrestling with so many feelings, mirrored by similar reactions from Black family members, friends, and community at large. I feel deep sadness at the loss of yet another beautiful life. I feel deep anger about the criminalization of the Black body that has led to so much hurt and death, and has also been leveraged as a form of power by some white people. I feel disgust toward comments that defend such deplorable behavior by suggesting a "different side to the story," victimizing the offenders, condemning Black people for our rightful reactions of anger, and denying larger systemic implications of anti-Black racism. I feel frustration as I hear well-meaning people suggest that these behaviors come from "bad apples," rather than doing the self-examination to understand the systemic nature of racism from which they are not exempt.

I feel anxiety as I brace myself for the inevitability of another precious Black life cut short in the future, and fear as I wonder whether a loved one or I will be next. I fight hopelessness as I see history on repeat from centuries ago, decades ago, years ago, and even weeks ago as I still mourn the recent senseless deaths of Ahmaud Arbery and Breonna Taylor.

And, I feel tired...tired of carrying the weight of all of this, tired of the constant trauma, and tired of the energy that I must expend to explain (and often prove) truths that seem obvious. That Black Lives Matter. It is challenging to integrate my feelings as a Black woman with my responsibilities as the leader of this organization. I often find myself drawing a line between "activist-Whitney" and "organizational-Whitney," when it comes to what I say and how I say it. I find myself asking:

- *Must I repeat something over and over again, even at the expense of my own emotional health?*

- *Should I water down my language for the sake of a more palatable reception, even at the expense of my truth?*
- *Will we lose supporters if I speak my truth?*
- *Will it even make a difference?*

Admittedly, at times, I have remained silent for the sake of preservation from the literal trauma that comes from sharing honestly. However, this time, I am speaking up:

- *I am speaking up because enough is enough. I am screaming in concert with many Black voices who are doing the same. We must be heard.*
- *I am speaking up because I understand the value of proximity. Our two organizational leaders are Black, and we are directly impacted by the daily toll of anti-Black racism. We believe in this work and it is personal. We show up to do this work despite its personal toll. We hope that this direct articulation of pain and conviction moves people to action.*
- *I am speaking up even though some people may respond negatively to this honesty. Racial justice often comes at the price of lost support. However, we have also experienced that despite such loss, we often gain allies with deeper commitment.*
- *I am speaking up because this is what our organization does. We engage allies. Instead of the more diluted message of dispersing a "toolkit" in response to the news headlines, our larger calling is for allyship to be employed as a way of life. Allyship means centering the hard truths from those who are directly impacted, and*

leveraging them as the basis to drive effective action.

- *I am speaking up because I have hope as I see Black people showing courage, strength, and demanding justice; as I see allies condemning racism, taking action, and recognizing the importance of both self-work and engaging others in these important conversations.*

I cling to this hope as we continue this difficult work. I have seen the power of calls for justice through institutional and personal transformation. It begins with acknowledging hard truths, and taking action accordingly. May we proceed today with a posture of both compassion and conviction, demanding change that is 400-plus years overdue.

I knew that the message was a risk. I knew that we would probably lose subscribers. And we did. Yet, an overwhelming number of responses were surprisingly compassionate and grateful for my honesty. Not a single response was that of fragility, and I was shocked. While the listserv audience was comprised of supporters who believed in the notion of allyship, history has shown me that such an audience does not exempt a Black woman from backlash when sharing her truth. All to say, the reaction was better than expected. I received many direct responses of genuine compassion and support. I hope that compassion transpires into conviction and a commitment to pursue justice moving forward—not pity.

I find myself navigating complex and contrasting emotions. On the one hand, I am hopeful as I see collective uprisings in cities across the country led by Black people, with solidarity from non-Black people. I have heard calls for defunding police and investment in community health, which I never could have expected outside of activist spaces even a mere month ago. I have seen local divestments from the carceral state and swift institutional action taken in a matter of days, which I would have otherwise expected to take decades to implement. For anyone who has ever questioned the value of protesting, let these times be an example. Direct action brings collective power to the people by giving them a voice. Direct action makes the masses listen, whether they want to or not. It forces decision-makers to act, even if solely from public pressure. It requires people to face disruption to their own routines and bubbles by saying, "If this continues to be our problem, then it will be your problem, too."

In my millennial life, I have not seen anything of this magnitude on a national level; and I am hopeful when I hear elders and baby boomer activists say the same, and that something feels different this time. How could I not be inspired by the people on whose shoulders I stand?

I feel deep sadness. I am saddened by the loss of yet another beautiful life, and for the loved ones who have experienced such a horrible tragedy. I am saddened for the Generation-Z Black youth, whose upbringing has been marked by video after video of Black bodies being brutally murdered. I am saddened by the fresh addition of trauma that may last forever in my body, and for the collective Black community as we witness yet another reminder that we systemically do not matter. I am saddened as I wonder whether we will ever systemically matter.

I have allowed myself to feel a deep rage toward the system and society. I could not help but ask, "Where was everyone before?" Do not get me wrong—I would rather people be late than never to their awakening and action. Still, the videos are not new. The outcries are not new. Why haven't people listened to us before? Why haven't people believed us before? What makes this different? What makes this more urgent? Anti-Black racism has been urgent in these lands for over 400 years. My anger is real, it is valid, and it is multi-faceted.

And lastly, I battle pessimism. I have heard a common narrative about how this moment could be the "tipping point"—that given the national uprising, the swift action, and the seemingly deepened commitment to anti-racism, we will ignite a change like never before. Yet, there have been uprisings before. Many times we have seen collective outrage, which then faded away when people were over it or something else took their attention. The only way that we will see a profound shift is if the conviction and action remain, deepen, and enhance. It will need to continue when the headlines fade, and when it is no longer trendy to protest. Only now does more of society think it is appropriate to say, "Black Lives Matter," after years of so many people finding the term divisive. Only now are so many more people and businesses willing to say, "Black Lives Matter," and post those signs on their windows when they had previously chosen silence under the argument of political neutrality. That, alone, has several implications. However, I will consider it progress. All Black lives will need to matter. Black lives will need to keep mattering. Black lives mattering will need to keep being others' priorities. It is critical to understand that centering Black lives gives us the strategies necessary for achieving liberation for everyone.

As this section time-shifts to present day a few years later, I reflect on my sentiments from that period and am disheartened by how my feelings remain the same. I recount the additional names to the list of Black people killed by police: Tony McDade, Rayshard Brooks, Casey

Goodson Jr., Andre Hill, Daunte Wright, Ma'Khia Bryant, Andrew Brown, Amir Locke, Patrick Lyoya, Jayland Walker, Tyre Nichols, Aaliyah Anders, Ryan Gainer, Roger Fortson, Sonya Massey, and a number of additional people that didn't make the headlines. Those are just a few of the higher-profile names, though none received the attention or outrage to the level of Floyd's murder.

I recount my horror on January 6 of 2021, while watching mainly white insurrectionists storm the Capitol to "take back power" and try to overturn Trump's 2020 election defeat. I hold back tears as I recall the murder of ten Black people in a Buffalo grocery store by an eighteen-year-old white supremacist, and I manage my frustration at the minimal coverage, outrage, and resources that the mass murder received compared to shootings in other non-Black communities in that same time period. I shudder when I think of the clips that I saw of Tyre Nichols's brutal murder, as he was beaten to death by police officers at a traffic stop—clips that I desperately tried avoiding, to no avail. My eyes well up with tears when comparing how both he and George Floyd wailed for their mothers as their lives were senselessly stripped away. I dissent into despair as I navigate the trauma and tragedy of another white supremacist mass shooting that killed three Black people in a Jacksonville Dollar General, and I am reminded of the cyclical and unending terror on Black people that has taken place for centuries. I shake my head at studies that show a sharp decrease in overall public support of the Movement for Black Lives since the 2020 uprising, and the loud "anti-DEI" sentiment across many institutions—including those that had previously espoused public and enthusiastic commitments.[37] The opposition, threat, and abandonment to both are even louder and more blatant since Trump's 2024 presidential re-election.

And I release a sigh, because none of this is surprising. Alongside the conversations of pain and rage with other Black people in 2020 was the collective knowledge that this supposed reckoning would not yield long-term systemic effects. I remember how I regularly heard white people in those periods say, "I am awakened by this, and I am now committed to anti-racism work for life!" I would often think to myself (and admittedly, sometimes say out loud in my exhaustion and low censor barrier), "Let's see in two years." Many Black people knew that when the headlines faded, when anti-racism was not trendy anymore, when actual risk and discomfort were required, and when the short-term focus needed to transition into a lifelong commitment, plenty of our claimed allies would abandon ship, slowly fade away, and/or remain silent and inactive. History and life have shown us that time and time again. Sadly, that season was no different.

As I reflect on the most recent 2024 election results, all of these ruminations feel just as fresh today as they did four years prior. I had been incredibly disturbed by how swiftly Trump had kept and grown his supporter base after his 2020 re-election defeat against President Biden, but I wasn't surprised. I had been hopeful about history being made by electing the first Black and Asian woman into the presidency with Vice President Harris's whirlwind candidacy, but I can't say that I ever thought it would happen. What surprised me most was how oddly calm I felt about the election outcome. As I processed, I realized that I had hit my lowest point regarding the implications of white supremacy's power in the year-long span between Trump's first election in 2016 (which did completely shock me) and the white supremacist gathering in Charlottesville that following summer.

A more poignant personal reflection was my lack of reaction to the implications about Black womanhood that were spotlit directly after Vice President Harris's defeat. As Black women publicly expressed valid agony and frustration about having to constantly show up collectively as this country's moral compass (just look at those election numbers by demographic), and about the misogynoir that continually demands our labor and perfection, but rejects our leadership and power, I agreed wholeheartedly with the narrative but had trouble accessing the emotion of the sentiment. I realized that it was because I had been operating at rock bottom for the past two years, after painfully realizing the impossible standards of Black women in leadership from running my own small organization. Of course they would be so forceful and glaring in respect to the highest position of power in the country. I had been navigating the realities of the election's underlying meaning for years, and this just felt like more data that demonstrated the systemic nature of it all. While the wounds never healed, I had learned to manage the pain for long enough that it had become my static state.

Still, my hope remains. I hope that some people were moved from the inside, out by the 2020 uprising for the long term. I hope that non-Black people will continue unlocking compassion as they witness and learn of anti-Black racism's pervasiveness and destruction. But compassion should be a catalyst for action. I hope that more people are willing to see and learn about the ubiquity of white supremacy and patriarchy, so that we have a larger collective group of truth-tellers speaking to what we are operating in, and what we should aspire toward. But knowing and speaking should also be catalysts for action, just like compassion. Action is the only way that any true shifts will come. People need to stay committed.

My hope remains because social justice work is rooted in it, and it is guided by an aspiration that we must constantly pursue. People will need to build on this commitment. This possibility counters my pessimism, and repositions me toward hope. That hope is what keeps me going. Hope is the fuel that keeps the flame of my idealism burning, because it speaks to possibility despite consistent evidence suggesting otherwise. Once hope is lost, all is lost, and there is still a lot to hope *and* work for.

CHAPTER 24

WE WERE BUILT FOR THIS

I discuss allyship excessively because I believe that white people have the most responsibility to do anti-racism work. We all need to unlearn the ways that white supremacy is deeply embedded in our society (and ourselves), *and* I am of the belief that white people hold the primary charge as the current beneficiaries and drivers of the system. Just to be clear, this is a charge based on responsibility, not pity or paternalism. Black folks are powerful.

The morning after Charlottesville, I attended my church back in the DC Metro area. My pastor had been on vacation out of the state, and he returned home late the night prior because he wanted to be there for his predominantly Black congregation after such traumatic events. I remember his inspirational sermon about the weekend, and toward the end he reminded us of a critical fact: "We were built for this."

Black people are powerful. Black people are beautiful. Black people are creative. Black people are amazing. I am reminded of this every time I see our perseverance in many forms throughout history in this country. From surviving the despicable theft and brutal voyage on slave ships; to the intolerable conditions of slavery's violence and working conditions; to the deplorable stripping and lack of civil rights through segregation; to the strategic implementation of "wars" on drugs and crime that continued locking us up and separating our families; to the continued criminalization of our existence through today's policing and legal system; to the daily weathering of our bodies and minds as we exist under this looming cloud of white supremacy. We are still here, we are still moving mountains, we are still shaking things up, we are still driving culture, and we are still demanding to be heard.

We were built for this because of our resilience. Resilience is in our DNA, literally. I see our resilience, not just in our demonstrated ability to persevere and disrupt amidst numerous efforts to keep us quiet and controlled; not just through enduring the continued evolution of our systemic marginalization; but also through our grace. It is the grace that we show every time we do not explode from the additional microaggressions at work and in public settings. It is the selflessness that we show as we support others' needs despite our continued disregard. It is the grace that we show by desiring equality and equity instead of revenge for the past 400-plus years.

We were built for this because our culture is everything. I love that amidst constant adversity, we have been able to develop such a unique and extensive way of being that connects us all. Black culture is so broad yet so inclusive. There is space in there for all of us. From our various forms of music, to our styles, to our dialects, to our movements, to our foods, to our expansive methods of cultivating community...we have our own world. It is a world from which *the* world draws inspiration, and then often ends up stealing or disrespecting. It is appropriated, and it is capitalized on. Many people seem to want to experience our culture, and then not acknowledge it or rectify our hardships. Many people are so accustomed to a society that extracts from Black people whatever and whenever they want, that they do the same with Black culture without batting an eye. There is a difference between honoring and appreciating, versus appropriating and stealing. Many people do the latter. While there is much more to say on that topic, my point is that our culture is that powerful, that beautiful, that magnetic, and that genius. Even though I hardly have any social media accounts, I prioritize my access to Black social media content (with much thanks to my loyal family and friends, who send me content to stay up with the times). Black social media demonstrates much of what I love about us. I can find everything that I need there: humor, critique, education, revolution, art, vocabulary, rage, joy, validation, acceptance, community, inspiration, hope, and home. Our culture is all of that. Our culture is everything, and I just love us.

We were built for this because we still have immeasurable joy. I laugh in my fullness around Black people. It comes straight from my gut, and from deep within my soul. I am continually impressed by the ways that we can make and find humor so creatively. Our stories, our entertainment, our parties...we can have a hard day, cut all the way up that night, and then get back to work the next morning. We can experience immense exuberance on the dance floor, at the concert, and in worship. We can fully entertain ourselves in a room or cookout of just us. We find joy in art. We find joy in humor. We find joy in community. We find joy in life.

We were built for this because we have each other. As much as white supremacy has literally tried to divide and separate us, our sense of community has remained strong. There are few things more sacred to me than intimate and uninterrupted community time. That foundation was instilled during my youth through nightly family dinners while growing up, family reunions during summertime, social mingling directly after church services, random pop-ins by friends, and weekly phone calls with loved ones. I see how those same habits have extended to my adulthood, and I am grateful for the intention with which my family instilled such a deep connection to community. That is how we have been able to create such beauty, and that is how we have been able to sustain it. As much as white-dominant culture has tried to steer society toward individualism, the Blackness that I know is intrinsically linked to collectivism and community. That is why we shut down the streets when one of us is killed by state-sanctioned violence. That is why we collectively celebrate when our youth get into colleges, or our coworkers get promotions. That is why we stop or stay late to help our colleagues get the tasks done. That is why we lend the money to friends and family members when they need support. That is why we root for everybody Black at the awards shows and in the competitions. We want us all to win.

We were built for this. We should not have to endure our systemic hardships, but it is telling that we have been able to do so and still dream, innovate, build, and celebrate. That doesn't mean that we lack internal challenges and areas for improvement. As humans, we will always have areas to grow. As communities, we will always have issues to work on. However, I reject the narrative that our community is broken and disconnected because I have only experienced the contrary. I cannot look at Black people and lack hope. My people give me hope. My ancestors give me hope. My community gives me hope. My family gives me hope. Black people give me hope, and make me positive that we will win.

CHAPTER 25

BEAUTY

Believe it or not, I am a very happy person. I have allowed myself to live into the "both, and, and all" that make up my complex personality and disposition as a Black woman. I have embraced the power and relief that come from speaking honestly, and knowing that it is valid. I have found value in expressing information that dwelled within me for years, and needed releasing. I have exhaled for the sake of my own health, and hopefully it has benefited at least some readers. These hard truths are motivated by my belief in society's potential. We must face the facts to achieve our possibilities. Those possibilities are beautiful, as are the many realities that I have witnessed in my everyday existence.

I have seen how history has made critical strides toward progress in human rights and racial justice. I am my ancestors' wildest dreams, and that is because they imagined, persevered, fought, and were not alone. There have always been so-called "radicals" and change-makers who were called to larger purposes than themselves, and were able to drive, inspire, and lead change.

I have seen allies show up and risk it all for the sake of justice. There will always be allies who truly live out the synonymous posture of accomplices and co-conspirators. I draw inspiration from their actions to inform my own avenues of effective solidarity and allyship in my areas of privilege.

I have seen people in positions of privilege, who were once ignorantly complicit, accept a humble posture of learning through discomfort. I have witnessed their transformation, and their active invitation of others to do the same.

I have seen tangible power and impact emerge from working together across different identities toward collective liberation. It reminds me that we really can do this.

I have seen Black people continue to be great. We cannot be stopped. We will not be stopped. No matter how dreary circumstances may seem, I always believe that we will win because we are just that amazing.

I have seen the beauty of deep and intentional community on small and large scales; people who pour fully into each other and are filled by mutual reciprocation.

And I have seen the transforming, healing, revolutionary, and unlimited power of love, with my parents as my shining example. I have received abundant and deep love from my parents since the moment that I left my mother's womb. I have witnessed willing sacrifice and selflessness from them that was never accompanied by resentment or burden. I have connected deeply to God's love through the example of spirituality that they set through their daily faith walks, and their nightly prayers over me. I have unlocked my own sense of empowered purpose, thanks to their constant motivation and encouragement of my gifts. I have experienced healing and safety from the harms of the world in their loving arms. I have seen the example of excellence through the bar that they set in their own lives and accomplishments. I have pursued ongoing growth by witnessing their posture of humility and charge to never stop learning. I have been deeply loved by them, and I have learned how to love others through them.

My parents model society's potential. The whole and thriving person that I can be is thanks to their continued covering and example. Their love motivates me to emulate as much of that as I can in my daily walk, and their characters are constant reminders that there is genuine good in the world. I can envision a fully liberated and just world, thanks in large part to my parents.

My journey is unique, and the result of countless experiences and people. The stories that I have shared are but a few of the thousands that exist in both my conscious and subconscious brain, framed in a manner that is hopefully of value—even if solely for the sake of my own outlet and another perspective to add to the mix. As I bring this narrative to a close, I wrestle with the most effective way to conclude. What parting words can complete a piece that is only a mere fraction of my many thoughts? What stories should I tell?

Should I tell the many stories of my grandparents, and the wisdom that they imparted on me through their own oral histories and admirable characters? My love for singing in the church was directly inspired by witnessing my late paternal grandmother's deep love for God and unabashed praise for God's blessings. One of my middle names honors the incredible woman that she was, and her servant's heart informed my own commitment to community as a core pillar of living out my faith. My passion and truth-telling are the direct genes of my maternal grandmother that coursed through my dynamic mother and into me. She has always stood firm in her convictions as the phenomenal woman that she is, and she regularly encouraged the same of me as I grew into the woman that I have become (she was also the first person to tell me that I would be a writer back in elementary school). My late maternal grandfather set the example for how one can embody resilience and joy as he told the stories of the barriers that he faced and broke in his military career, yet he had infinite jokes and laughs to share with us in every interaction. I share his middle name, and strive to exude the same outstanding character and energy that he modeled. And my late paternal grandfather was an amazing man of wisdom and respect, who I never met but whose spirit of integrity and protection radiates through my father's demeanor, who carries his namesake. I carry his legacy with pride and responsibility. All of them were vessels of power and love, and elders whose genes I am honored to carry.

Should I tell the story of how my parents attended every game, performance, event, and competition while I was growing up? It even became a running joke with teachers, classmates, and teammates to find my parents in the audience by identifying my mom's large video camera. Their supportive presence at every life moment remains consistent to this day.

Should I tell the story of the vastly different personalities shared between my sisters and me, yet how we have remained the best of friends? I speak to at least one of them on a daily basis, and they consistently inspire me with their kindness, grace, and brilliance. I truly do not know where I would be without my literal sister-friends.

Should I tell the story about the time that my high school close friend and neighbor ran to our house and sat on my family's rooftop with a bat, when we thought it was being intruded while my younger sisters were home alone? He was willing to risk his own safety without any hesitation to protect my dear little siblings, and I am grateful that everyone remained safe that night amidst the false alarm.

Should I tell the stories of the many laughs, debates, and tears shared amongst our small but tight Black community in college? That was my first personal and intimate experience with the beauty and power of the Black diaspora and community, as we gathered from various backgrounds to form our strong and loyal bond. Some of my closest friends came from those college days.

Should I tell the story about my church vocal director, who not only coached me to unlock my best musicianship, but also lovingly called me his daughter and was one of my fiercest protectors? Amazingly, dozens of people on my Praise and Worship team can speak to a similar relationship, and his recent passing continues to remind me to love excessively and abundantly every day, as set by his example.

Should I tell the story of the generous supporter who funded my debut album through his charity label? My childhood dream of dropping an album was achieved through his benevolence, with the sole motivation of supporting my creative endeavors and amplifying my voice (literally).

Should I tell the story of my church music director, the most talented musician that I know, who graciously agreed to fully produce my first album? He brought my dream and vision to life, and I know that such an intensive act of service with his incredible gift was out of commitment to our friendship.

Should I tell the stories about how there was a years-long period where my close friends and loved ones checked on me anytime there was a local protest? They even went on active searches to find me when I had not responded to texts or calls, out of concern that my activism may have led to danger.

Should I tell the story of how liberators, allies, and co-conspirators did the electric slide and the wobble as we held down downtown DC the year after Charlottesville, when white nationalists tried to come to the city to hold another rally? Not only would they not take over the city, but they would not take our joy that year, either.

Should I tell the stories of the numerous Black-women squads and besties that I have had throughout every season of my adult life as supporters during the lowest of lows, and cheerleaders during the highest of highs? I reject the lie that we only tear each other down because my whole life has overflowed with their steadfast loyalty.

Should I tell the story of the hundreds of Black elders who have poured their wisdom into me, willingly taken me under their wings, gone to bat for me, opened doors for me, lovingly guided me in my decisions, and explained the lessons to me in my missteps? At the heart of our community is deep love, fierce protection, and knowledge that spans across generations.

Should I tell the story of how each of my immediate family members shared their unwavering support for me when I decided to leave my secure job to start a nonprofit organization? Amidst plenty of external criticism and doubt that I faced in the startup journey, their love, prayers, and encouragement were loudest as they backed my motivation to build the vision that I had in my head.

Should I tell the story of how a close friend joined me as a cofounder and then a coworker for the organization that I started, as both a teammate and an ally? I will be infinitely grateful for the unique season of a collaborative work environment rooted in friendship.

Should I tell the story of how a Black woman friend and fellow organizational leader saw my urgent need for a break from the eight years of arduous work, and donated a "sabbatical grant" to our non-profit—out of her own organization's budget—so that I could take off over two months to rest and heal? Her gesture of support and generosity is one of the many that I have received and witnessed from other Black leaders, which inspires me to follow in their footsteps of abundance and community.

Should I tell the story of how my mentor road-tripped with me (and drove the whole time) so that I could safely get to my family's home during the pandemic, and dropped himself off at the airport upon destination arrival to fly back to his own family—all within the same day? He has consistently been one of the most supportive people in my life, and has always been available for guidance, time, encouragement, and support.

Should I tell the story of how I was blessed to spend almost two years of deep quality time with my family while I quarantined with them during most of the COVID-19 pandemic? I am so grateful that, amidst such a tragic and terrifying period, I was able to spend time with them that I never could have dreamed of having in my adult years. I'm also appreciative of my parents' generosity in warmly welcoming me to stay in their home for as long as I wanted.

Should I tell the story of laughing so hard that I could not breathe during multiple games of Catch Phrase, Pictionary, Spades, and trivia with my family? We have laughed that much together at the dinner table, in the family room, and on road trips throughout my entire life. So much of my joy and hope come from the smiles, love, encouragement, and fun that consistently filled the household.

These are individual stories of beauty, happiness, loyalty, community, love, and hope that I experience regularly. Yes, there are hardships, injustices, and pain; but support, thriving, and possibility regularly surround me. When the challenges feel too big, I reflect on these stories to remind me of what this is all for. Breathe in, breathe out, and continue moving forward. There is nowhere else to pursue but forward.

ENDNOTES

1 Angelou, Maya. *Letter to My Daughter*. New York: Random House, 2009.

2 "Adultification Bias." Center on Gender Justice and Opportunity at Georgetown Law. Accessed July 11, 2024. https://genderjusticeandopportunity.georgetown.edu/focus-areas/adultification-bias.

3 Asare, Janice Gassam. "Why Does Everything Have To Be About Race?" *Forbes*. October 28, 2021. https://www.forbes.com/sites/janicegassam/2021/10/28/why-does-everything-have-to-be-about-race/.

4 Planas, Antonio. "Blacks, Latinos and Native Americans Disproportionally Killed by Covid-19 Last Year, Study Says." *NBC News*. October 5, 2021. https://www.nbcnews.com/news/us-news/blacks-latinos-native-americans-disproportionally-killed-covid-19-last-year-n1280837.

5 "Why Lead with Race? Challenging Institutional Racism to Create an Equitable Society for All." City of Seattle Official Website. Racial and Social Justice Initiative. Accessed July 9, 2024. https://www.seattle.gov/documents/Departments/RSJI/why-lead-with-race.pdf.

6 Davidson, Kizha. "Why We Use BIPOC." *YWCA* (blog), March 12, 2024. https://www.ywcaworks.org/blogs/ywca/tue-03122024-1000/why-we-use-bipoc.

7 Carrillo, Sequoia, and Pooja Salhotra. "The US Student Population Is More Diverse, But Schools Are Still Highly Segregated." *NPR*. July 14, 2022. https://www.npr.org/2022/07/14/1111060299/school-segregation-report.

8 Rothstein, Richard. *The Color of Law: A Forgotten History of How Our Government Segregated America*. New York: Liveright Publishing, 2017.

9 Weller, Christian. "Racial Wealth Inequality Stays High In A Strong Economy." *Forbes*. February 1, 2024. www.forbes.com/sites/christianweller/2024/02/01/racial-wealth-inequality-stays-high-in-strong-economy.

10 "The Origins of Modern Day Policing." National Association for the Advancement of Colored People. Accessed July 11, 2024. www.naacp.org/find-resources/history-explained/origins-modern-day-policing.

11 Ghandnoosh, Nazgol. "Report: One in Five: Ending Racial Inequity in Incarceration." The Sentencing Project. October 11, 2023. www.sentencingproject.org/reports/one-in-five-ending-racial-inequity-in-incarceration.

12 Budd, Kristen M. "Report: Private Prisons in the United States." The Sentencing Project. February 21, 2024. www.sentencingproject.org/reports/private-prisons-in-the-united-states.

13 Ross, Janell. "Dedrick Asante-Muhammad Won't Sugarcoat Wealth Disparity." *Time*. February 1, 2024. www.time.com/collection/closers/6564912/dedrick-asante-muhammad.

14 Perry, Andre M., Hannah Stephens, and Manann Donoghoe. "Black Wealth Is Increasing, But So Is the Racial Wealth Gap." The Brookings Institution. January 9, 2024. www.brookings.edu/articles/

black-wealth-is-increasing-but-so-is-the-racial-wealth-gap.

15 King, Dr. Martin Luther. "Awake Through a Great Revolution." Speech. National Cathedral, Washington, DC, March 31, 1968.

16 King, Dr. Martin Luther. "A Proper Sense of Priorities." Speech. New York Avenue Presbyterian Church, Washington, DC, February 6, 1968.
King, Dr. Martin Luther. "Letter from Birmingham Jail." American Friends Service Committee, 1963.
King, Dr. Martin Luther. "I Have a Dream." Speech. Lincoln Memorial, Washington, DC, August 28, 1963.

17 Aggeler, Madeleine. "A Black Man Asked a White Woman to Leash Her Dog. She Called the Cops." *The Cut*. May 28, 2020. https://www.thecut.com/2020/05/amy-cooper-central-park-dog-video.html.

18 Delgado, Richard, and Jean Stefancic. *Critical Race Theory: An Introduction*. Fourth edition. New York: New York University Press, 2023.

19 Guynn, Jessica. "White Women Benefit Most from Affirmative Action. So Why Do They Oppose It?" *USA Today*. June 30, 2023. www.usatoday.com/story/money/2023/06/29/affirmative-action-who-benefits-white-women/70371219007.

20 "Being an African American 'Superwoman' Might Come with a Price." American Heart Association. February 11, 2020. www.heart.org/en/news/2020/02/11/being-an-african-american-superwoman-might-come-with-a-price.

21 Biewin, John. "Season 2, Episode 3: Made in America." Produced by Scene on Radio. March 16, 2017. Podcast. MP3 audio. 33:39. https://sceneonradio.org/episode-33-made-in-america-seeing-white-part-3/.

22 Jones, Kenneth and Tema Okun. *Dismantling Racism: A Workbook for Social Change Groups*. ChangeWork. 2001.

23 Suarez, Kerrien, and Whitney Parnell. "'We Specialize in the Wholly Impossible': Navigating Three Black Women Tropes in

Leadership." *Nonprofit Quarterly Magazine 31*, no. 1 (2024). https://nonprofitquarterly.org/we-specialize-in-the-wholly-impossible-navigating-three-black-women-tropes-in-leadership.

24 "The other half of the time, I could see the fragility rising." DiAngelo, Robin. *White Fragility: Why It's So Hard for White People to Talk About Racism*. Boston: Beacon Press, 2018.

25 King, Dr. Martin Luther. "Letter from Birmingham Jail." American Friends Service Committee, 1963.

26 Fernando, Christine. "Emboldened 'manosphere' accelerates threats and demeaning language toward women after US election." AP News. November 30, 2024.

27 Geronimus, Arline. *Weathering: The Extraordinary Stress of Ordinary Life in an Unjust Society*. New York: Little, Brown, 2023.

28 Ibid.

29 Brown, Ashley. "'Least Desirable'? How Racial Discrimination Plays Out in Online Dating." *NPR*. January 9, 2018. www.npr.org/2018/01/09/575352051/least-desirable-how-racial-discrimination-plays-out-in-online-dating.

30 Transcript. *Citizen King*. PBS. https://www.pbs.org/wgbh/americanexperience/films/mlk/#transcript.

31 Crenshaw, Kimberlé. "Demarginalizing the Intersection of Race and Sex: A Black Feminist Critique of Anti-Discrimination Doctrine, Feminist Theory, and Antiracist Politics." *The University of Chicago Legal Forum 140* (1989): 25-42.

32 "Manifesto." Landback Organization. Accessed July 11, 2024. www.landback.org/manifesto.

33 "Voting Laws Roundup: May 2024." Brennan Center for Justice. May 17, 2024. www.brennancenter.org/our-work/research-reports/voting-laws-roundup-may-2024.

34 King, Dr. Martin Luther. "Letter from Birmingham Jail." American Friends Service Committee, 1963.

35 Malcolm X. Speech. Los Angeles, California, May 22, 1962.

36 Lorde, Audre. "The Master's Tools Will Never Dismantle the Master's House." 1984. *Sister Outsider: Essays and Speeches.* Berkeley: Crossing Press, 2007.

37 Horowitz, Juliana Menasce, Kiley Hurst, and Dana Braga. "Support for the Black Lives Matter Movement Has Dropped Considerably From Its Peak in 2020." Pew Research Center. June 14, 2023. www.pewresearch.org/social-trends/2023/06/14/support-for-the-black-lives-matter-movement-has-dropped-considerably-from-its-peak-in-2020.

SUGGESTED READING

Collected below are the books mentioned throughout the text of *Breathing Out*, collated here for ease of reference.

- *The New Jim Crow: Mass Incarceration in the Age of Colorblindness* by Michelle Alexander
- *Letter to My Daughter* by Maya Angelou
- *I'm Still Here: Black Dignity in a World Made for Whiteness* by Austin Channing Brown
- *Eloquent Rage: A Black Feminist Discovers Her Superpower* by Brittney Cooper
- *Why Are All the Black Kids Sitting Together in the Cafeteria?: And Other Conversations About Race* by Beverly Daniel Tatum
- *Critical Race Theory: An Introduction* by Richard Delgado and Jean Stefancic

- *White Fragility: Why It's So Hard for White People to Talk About Racism* by Robin DiAngelo
- *Biased: Uncovering the Hidden Prejudice That Shapes What We See, Think, and Do* by Jennifer Eberhardt
- *Weathering: The Extraordinary Stress of Ordinary Life in an Unjust Society* by Arline Geronimus
- *The 1619 Project: A New Origin Story* by Nikole Hannah-Jones
- *Rest Is Resistance: A Manifesto* by Tricia Hersey
- *Black Women Taught Us* by Jenn M. Jackson
- *This Will Be My Undoing: Living at the Intersection of Black, Female, and Feminist in (White) America* by Morgan Jerkins
- *Sister Outsider: Essays and Speeches* by Audre Lorde
- *They Said This Would be Fun: Race, Campus Life, and Growing Up* by Eternity Martis
- *The Sum of Us: What Racism Costs Everyone and How We Can Prosper Together* by Heather McGhee
- *So You Want to Talk About Race* by Ijeoma Oluo
- *White Women Cry and Call Me Angry: A Black Woman's Memoir on Racism in Philanthropy* by Yanique Redwood
- *The Color of Law: A Forgotten History of How Our Government Segregated America* by Richard Rothstein
- *A More Perfect Union: A New Vision for Building the Beloved Community* by Adam Russell Taylor
- *Me and White Supremacy* by Layla Saad
- *Just Mercy* by Bryan Stevenson
- *Caste: The Origins of Our Discontents* by Isabel Wilkerson

- *Black Fatigue: How Racism Erodes the Mind, Body, and Spirit* by Mary-Frances Winters

ABOUT THE AUTHOR

Whitney Parnell is a Black millennial activist, singer, and nonprofit leader. An alumna of Washington University in St. Louis, she founded Service Never Sleeps in 2015, a Black-led racial justice nonprofit. Parnell is also a musician, and released a social justice album in 2022 called *What Will You Do?*

Parnell was the lead researcher and author for Service Never Sleeps' 2024 report, *What Does It Mean to Be Black-Led?: An Extensive Guide on Liberatory Organizational Management, Black Leaders' Experiences, and Their Needs from Supporters to Thrive.* This is her first book.